P9-CEM-374

Chris,
Remember to
visit your
homeless!
—Paul

LEADERSHIP ON DEMAND

HOW SMART CEO'S TAP INTERIM MANAGEMENT TO DRIVE REVENUE

By Charles Besondy and Paul Travis
Edited by Theresa Heath

LOD Publishing, LLC

Leadership on Demand
How Smart CEO's Tap Interim Management to Drive Revenue

By Charles Besondy and Paul Travis
Edited by Theresa Heath

Published by LOD Publishing, LLC
3720 Gattis School Road
#800-231
Round Rock, Texas 78664
http://www.leadership-on-demand.com

ISBN 978-0-9802035-1-6

ACKNOWLEDGMENTS

CHARLES BESONDY

The following executives graciously gave me their time and insight, which made this book possible: David Altounian, serial entrepreneur, over-achiever, friend and client; Rick Krause, one of the "smart" CEO's whom I admire greatly for his management skill; William Leake, an inspiration to many, always eager to serve and a man who never saw a word he didn't like; and Freddie Carroll, an investor with kindness, grace, a big smile and a low golf handicap.

This project would not have been possible without the immeasurable contribution and advice from my authoring and editing partners, Paul and Theresa.

A special acknowledgment is extended to the program leaders, fellow coaches, and participants in my Landmark Education community who stood for the possibility of this book.

And no acknowledgment would be complete without expressing my gratitude for God's blessing that guided every word and decision.

PAUL TRAVIS

Having begun, but not completed, the process of writing two other books, I would first like to acknowledge and appreciate my authoring and editing partners, for the rewarding collaboration and helping me get over the finish line, bringing an untold story to light.

Next, I thank the people who shared their insights and allowed me to get into their thought process: Alfred den Besten, Dr. John Castle, Brad Furber, and Bill Sequeira.

Finally and above all, I extend deep appreciation to my wife, Nancy, and our children (Savannah and Gabriel) for their patience as I told them far too many times, "Just another couple hours and I'll finish these chapters!"

THERESA HEATH

I would like to thank my colleagues; Chuck, for his leadership on the project and for inviting me to join him in this endeavor, and Paul, for his insight, enthusiasm and diligence.

I would also express my gratitude to Jack Lazard, Jim Grogan and all the other experts and advisers who contributed their knowledge and wisdom; your input has been instrumental in creating this body of work.

And finally, to my husband Brady and daughters Madison and Lauren; thank you for your support and acceptance of the time invested in this book.

CONTENTS

INTRODUCTION

FILLING THE PERFORMANCE VACUUM

By Charles Besondy

A DAY IN THE LIFE

On her way to work, Mia Turner knew it was going to be an important day. She was just three weeks into her new role as VP of Marketing for Solid Software Objects, and today she was going to see the first signs of her impact. As her car nosed along in heavy traffic, she ran her day's schedule through her mind. It was a big day and she was optimistic; she had been in this situation many times before.

The survey results due on her desk by 9:00 AM would tell her how the new positioning strategy was playing out. Her 10 o'clock was with the VP of Sales to finalize the new sales and lead generation process they had created together. At 11 o'clock she was meeting with the company's CRM platform vendor to inform them of her department's functional requirements for the soon-to-be implemented system.

Lunch today would be with senior staff; the CEO, COO, CTO, and CIO. It was her turn to present some preliminary ideas on the company's growth strategy.

On tap for this afternoon's marketing staff meeting: her department heads would be delivering the first reports in a new dashboard format that she had implemented. She and other executives would now see monthly performance reports that showed Marketing's contribution to revenue, key customer acquisition, customer satisfaction and referral, and cost per acquisition—all of which were key business metrics important to Solid Software Objects.

She had set aside two hours at the end of the day to work on employee evaluations that were coming due soon. Mia's dinner would be with the president of one of the three Web marketing firms her team was reviewing.

Yes, it was going to be a high-performance day; day number 16 to be exact.

Walking into her office and looking at her watch she smiled; funny how the sense of urgency never left her. Indeed, at Solid Software Objects she had only 85 days remaining and then she'd be gone. Mia Turner, VP of Marketing, is an interim manager.

A DEFINITION OF INTERIM MANAGEMENT

So what is *interim management*? We found a definition on Wikipedia that is as clear and concise as any.

> *"Interim management is the temporary provision of additional management resources and skills. Interim management can be seen as the short-term assignment of a proven heavyweight interim executive manager to manage a period of transition, crisis or change within a company. In this situation, a permanent role may be unnecessary or impossible to find at short notice. Additionally, there may be nobody internally who is suitable for, or available to take up, the position in question."*

In addition, we would add that an interim manager is <u>not</u> someone who is working temporarily to pay the bills while they search for a full-time position. Interim managers are interim managers by choice, even if occasionally they may be lured by an extraordinary opportunity to join an organization as a full-time executive.

We'd also add that an interim is usually paid by the day, under a contract, to achieve certain results. This means the interim can function in strategic or operational capacities, or both.

Finally, we'd like to note that the use of interim managers is not limited to VP's and C-level executives. Actually, interims are frequently called upon to fill gaps at director-level or group-level positions, too.

BECAUSE YOUR WORLD CHANGES WITH EVERY BLINK

Where would business be without the Mia's of the world, those highly versatile and capable executives who can step into one company after another and make a difference quickly?

We can tell you; they'd be under-performing. Frankly, many companies, even successful ones, are under-performing to some degree for the simple reason that they attempt to fill every sales and marketing executive resource with a full-time employee (FTE) and then wonder why every 24-36 months or so they're considering replacing the individual.

Look around you. Your business environment is simply too sporadic and too fluid to chain your company's revenue engine (sales and marketing) to an old-fashioned "hire for career" philosophy.

Your company's mission statement may very well embody "hire for career" and "develop from within" principles, but that sort of rhetoric is a carryover from the 1950's and 1960's. Today a company is under tremendous pressure to swap out, or "reassign" a senior executive or department head at the earliest sign that the person "doesn't have what it takes anymore."

Therein lays the biggest challenge to maintaining company performance. Many sales and marketing executives can be deemed inadequate at any given point in time because the market changes too dramatically and too frequently. It's nearly impossible to accurately foresee what training a sales or marketing executive is going to need in order to meet the whip-saw changes in the market place.

TWO YEARS IN A LIFE

By now you may be nodding your head in agreement, or wondering where in the world we got such ideas. Much of this book is based on the observations of its authors who together have over 75 years of sales and marketing management experience in various companies both big and small. Other sources of insight came from the executives we interviewed for the book. Therefore, what we're presenting is a picture of the world seen through our eyes based on real-world experiences and observations.

Your experience to-date may be entirely different than what we're depicting in the graphs and discussion below. However, we anticipate most readers are going to recognize and relate to the situations we're about to describe.

Figure 1 illustrates a typical life cycle for a Sales or Marketing leader in any industry segment that is evolving rapidly, such as technology. The line depicts

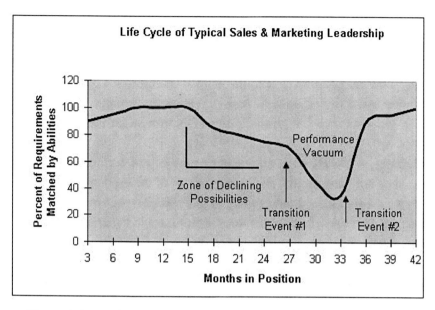

Figure 1: Loss of Momentum and Performance

how well the executive's skills and experience meet the requirements of the business environment over time.

If the candidate was a good hire, he will step into the company and perform well within three months, gaining knowledge of the organization and products, and be at 100% performance level within nine months or less. At the point leading up to the individual's anniversary date, things are going well. The executive is meeting or exceeding his goals and the CEO is feeling very good about the decision to bring this person on.

This level of high performance and high management satisfaction can last for another three to six months, but so often the executive's second year in the position is much rougher. Why a "rock star" one quarter and a manager on the bubble the next? Often it is because there is a change in the business environment that the executive is not able to adjust to, or simply doesn't see. What worked last year, isn't working now. The changes can be external, such as shifts in consumer purchase behaviors, or internal, such as a merger that alters the organization's culture.

In the diagram's Zone of Declining Possibilities, the executive is struggling to understand this new business environment and adopt fresh strategies, but the CEO and the Board are getting impatient. If the situation can't be turned around, at about month 27, the executive is asked to leave.

The Zone of Declining Possibilities represents a period of about a year when the company's business and revenue momentum is declining and opportunity costs are increasing. This is a result of the key sales or marketing executive no longer being an ideal match for the challenges of the current business environment.

Unfortunately, in this scenario, missed opportunities and declining momentum have only just started. Following the exit of the executive (Transition Event #1 in the diagram), the company begins to define its requirements for a replacement and start the search. In the meantime, others in the organization scramble to pick up the slack. The company slips into the Performance Vacuum.

The Performance Vacuum is typically the three to nine month period during which the search, recruitment and negotiation process for a new FTE occurs. It ends when the new executive is hired at Transition Event #2, and the cycle starts anew.

This scenario certainly doesn't occur in *every* company every two or three years, but it is our experience that it happens in a very high percentage of companies.

There are those rare executives that have the ability to stay one step ahead of an evolving business environment, but they are the exception and not the rule.

Look again at the diagram in Figure 1: out of the 42 months in the time-line, just 12 months see a 100% match of executive ability to the requirements of the business environment. For another 12 months, the performance is 90% to 95%. The remaining 18 months see declining performance, typically represented by a loss of market momentum, declining rate of revenue growth, and an increase in missed market opportunities.

The chart for the sales and marketing executives in your organization may be different. Perhaps the cycle is longer, or the periods of decline shallower; however as a general rule there are periods of declining performance and momentum of three to nine months that if managed differently can yield incremental performance gains.

In this fluid business environment, how can a CEO <u>consistently</u> maintain company momentum and performance when the engine for that performance is the skill-set and experience of his key sales and marketing people? How can declining business results be mitigated in the Zone of Declining Possibilities and the Performance Vacuum?

Smart CEO's are not letting gaps in critical skill-set and bandwidth slow down their company's performance or limit the opportunities it takes on. That's because they've learned to add interim executives to their resource arsenal.

Figure 2 illustrates the potential impact of continually selecting interim

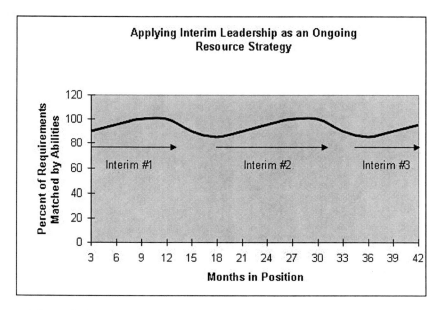

Figure 2: Serial Application of Interim Talent

executives to match the business situation at hand. This strategy avoids the deep declines and valleys common with a full-time employee strategy. In this example, Interim #1 comes on-board and uses his knowledge and leadership to carry the company forward for 12-18 months. Every year or so, the company assesses its sales and marketing leadership requirements and brings in a different interim (or retains the incumbent), to hold the reins for the coming year. If done systematically, the company shouldn't experience prolonged periods of declining performance.

Your time line certainly might vary; you may wish to re-evaluate interims every nine months, for instance.

6

If you don't choose to adopt a serial interim strategy, as depicted in Figure 2, consider using interims to avoid the occasional Performance Vacuum. Figure 3 illustrates the potential impact of using an interim to fill a gap while a search for a full-time employee is being conducted. Compare Figure 3 with Figure 1 and you can clearly see the potential for maintaining business momentum with this strategy.

This book explores how and why business leaders are waking up to the potential of deploying interim managers in sales and marketing. The wise use of interim leadership on the revenue side enables them to maintain a high level of business performance.

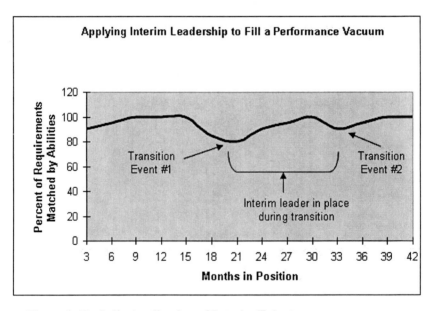

Figure 3: Periodic Application of Interim Talent

A RICH RESOURCE POOL: BABY BOOMERS TO THE RESCUE

Contributing to the problem of inconsistent performance is the scarcity of management talent. In July 2007, *The Economist,* in association with CIT Group Inc., published a report that analyzed the economic outlook for U.S. middle-market companies (by their definition, companies from $25MM to $1B annual revenue). An excerpt from the *Perspectives from America's Economic Engine: US Middle Market Outlook 2007* paints a disheartening picture:

> *"When it comes to obstacles to growth, a shortage of talented staff is cited most frequently (35%), followed by labour costs (25%) and market saturation (25%). The lack of high calibre staff is especially felt by the healthcare and IT industries."*

According to Manpower's 2007 Talent Shortage Survey, "Management/Executive" is the 5th-toughest job category for employers to fill, due to a shortage of qualified candidates. *Forty-one percent* of U.S. companies surveyed reported having difficulty filling management positions.

Partially offsetting the lack of talent for full-time hire is a growing pool of executives who are serving, by choice, the last 5-15 years of their careers as interim, "just-in-time" executives. Unfortunately, nobody knows how many interim leaders are available to take your call in the U.S. (See Chapter 8 on finding interim talent). As a point of reference, the U.K. interim provider firm, Russam GMS, estimates that in the U.K. there are 10,000 to 20,000 interim managers.

WHY THIS BOOK

Your authors are experienced executives and have been providing interim leadership services for large and small companies. We know the benefits. We also see the lack of understanding and the initial resistance to the concept. While books have been written for interim managers, we saw a clear need for a text written for CEO's and Board members to help them evaluate and adopt the concept.

In a world where outsourcing is commonplace, contract employees exist in nearly every area and entire departments, such as HR or Engineering, are outsourced or contracted, why is top management not seeing the same opportunity with sales and marketing leadership positions? Interim CIO's, COO's and CFO's proliferate. Why not CMO's and CSO's? Why not VP of Marketing and VP of Sales? Why not Director of Marketing and Director of Sales Operations as interim positions? Why suffer through the Zone of Declining Possibilities and the Performance Vacuum when you can continually match the challenges of the marketplace with the ideal set of skills and experience?

Whether you adopt interim management as a long-term repetitive solution or to fill a one-time gap, it is an alternative strategy that warrants serious consideration without bias from "the way we've always done it".

Leadership on Demand was a collaborative effort of three interim executives. We each conducted interviews, contributed chapters, and brought ideas to the table from our experience as interims, consultants, and full-time executives. One of us, Theresa Heath, is a strategist and sales leader; Paul Travis and Charles Besondy are marketing leaders. You'll notice that the book has been edited to preserve the different styles of its respective authors.

We believe that the ideas and best practices presented in this book will create a healthy dialogue about the use of interim leaders in sales and marketing functions—a discussion that can only lead to the adoption of more versatile management resource strategies to elevate business performance.

1.

KNOWING WHEN IT'S TIME FOR AN ALTERNATIVE SOLUTION

By Charles Besondy

One early-warning signal that an interim management solution is warranted within your company is when you start rationalizing why opportunities can't be addressed, or objectives not achieved.

You may feel as though you're trying to out-maneuver the competition with a family sedan rather than a Maserati. Or you may sense that you're constantly making Solomon-like decisions about which business opportunities your team has the bandwidth to attack all the while worried that more nimble competitors will beat you to the prize.

The following situations routinely arise in organizations both large and small. Each situation can be successfully and cost-effectively addressed with interim or on-demand leadership in sales and marketing.

1. A significant revenue or marketing event is in jeopardy
2. Totally new strategies or programs must be implemented or tested
3. A gap exists in a key position
4. A specific skill set is needed, but not permanently
5. Additional bandwidth needed, but not permanently
6. Objectivity in a leadership position would be beneficial, especially during strategic planning
7. Hands-on coaching and training is required to elevate skill and process knowledge of existing staff

While it's true that consulting firms can be retained for some of these situations, the cost of an interim manager is generally far less. In addition, the loyalties of an interim are more closely aligned with the client, particularly if the interim leader's compensation is tied to performance versus a consulting firm's focus on billable hours. (See chapter 10).

A SIGNIFICANT REVENUE OR MARKETING EVENT IS IN JEOPARDY

Of the seven situations mentioned, a significant revenue event is one that many CEO's don't immediately see as suitable for an interim management assignment. However, the short-term, one-time nature of this problem is well-suited to an interim leadership solution.

Keep in mind that interim leaders are highly experienced, senior-level executives. They aren't fresh MBAs. Due to in-depth experience in a particular discipline or industry, an interim manager can quickly and objectively assess the obstacles to achieving your business target, and unlike a consultant, actually step in to make it happen.

One-time revenue events can include an upcoming valuation, fiscal year-end or a pending merger in which hitting a revenue target carries additional significance. You may also want to consider interim management for business development or corporate development roles.

> *"A lot of companies can't afford biz-dev or corp-dev employees on a full-time basis. Yet there are interim leaders who have this expertise and can apply it to 2, 3, or 4 clients more effectively and at a cheaper cost on an outsourced basis."*
> --Brad Furber, President, Xeriton Corporation

One-time marketing events typically include major product introductions, strategic planning and pricing. The tendency here is to first look for help from a consulting firm or agency. However, if your company lacks the necessary marketing leadership to direct and manage the consultant/agency, the end result can miss the mark in a very expensive way.

For many enlightened CEO's, the better solution is to bring interim managers into the company to operate at strategic and tactical levels to: make the product introduction a success, provide wisdom and objectivity to the planning process or create market-centric positioning and pricing strategies. The interim leader can give the company the "shot in the arm" it needs, elevate the skill-level of the permanent employees in the marketing department and leave when the event has passed.

NEW STRATEGIES OR PROGRAMS MUST BE IMPLEMENTED OR TESTED

Companies, especially market leaders, are constantly tweaking their sales and marketing processes. This frequently involves implementing or testing programs and strategies that are new to the organization. We all know stories of promising strategies that fell victim to inept execution or were flawed from the beginning due to management myopia.

If your company is embarking on a new strategy or testing a new program, be honest about the organization's ability to pull it off. Increase the likelihood of success by bringing in an interim manager who has experience in the strategy or program you're about to test.

> *"I've learned that interim leaders in marketing are particularly useful when we're implementing a type of marketing strategy or tactic that is completely new to us. Search marketing was a recent example. We knew that paid search and natural search would be critical to iTaggit's success, but our knowledge was light in the area at that time. So when we brought in an interim VP Marketing to put our launch plan together for us, knowledge of search was a requirement. It helped us to be successful much faster."*
> -- David Altounian, CEO, iTaggit.com

A GAP EXISTS IN A KEY POSITION

Sales and marketing executives come and go. Department directors come and go. When a gap exists in a leadership position the company's performance is handicapped. This is an ideal time to have an interim manager fill the position and maintain momentum while the recruitment process for a permanent executive progresses. (Chapter 4 is devoted to this topic).

> *"When a company has a gap in a key position, it must calculate the opportunity cost for the 3-6 months it'll take to fill that position. The cost is almost always greater than the fee for an interim manager to fill the gap."*
> --William Leake, CEO, Apogee Search

A SPECIFIC SKILL SET IS NEEDED, BUT NOT PERMANENTLY

This is one of the more common situations leading to an interim management engagement. For example, you recognize that your sales team needs training, but the skills don't exist inside the organization. Let's say a move from direct sales to channel sales is required, but that channel expertise doesn't reside within your company.

The first tendency is to pick up the phone and call a consulting firm, but an interim manager makes more sense if you can locate one with the right background. The cost will be less and you'll have someone who is a more objective extension of your management team.

As part of the engagement scope, you should also request that the interim leader present a recommendation stating whether or not the skill is required within your company permanently.

Sometimes the question isn't one-time or permanent; rather it's full-time or part-time. An interim manager can be the one-time solution or the part-time solution.

> *"It's a relatively easy decision to select an interim A-player rather than a permanent, distracted C-player trying to wear multiple hats."*
> --William Leake, CEO, Apogee Search

ADDITIONAL BANDWIDTH NEEDED, BUT NOT PERMANENTLY

Occasionally, specific skills aren't in short supply at your company, bandwidth is. It is not uncommon to see an important initiative--annual strategic planning, a national sales conference, a product launch or the formulation of a product strategy to name few-- threatened because your team is fully engaged with day-to-day, revenue-generating activities. These situations are ideal for an on-demand leader to step in and lend a hand for several months.

What's more, you can decide to place the interim on the new initiative or on the day-to-day activities in order to free up the permanent staff to address the new initiative.

Smart CEO's put the right amount of wood behind the arrowhead by using on-demand leaders.

OBJECTIVITY IN LEADERSHIP

If you observe that the annual planning process at your company is becoming too inbred, perhaps too myopic, add an interim leader with suitable credentials and experience to the team. The fresh insight and perspective, combined with objectivity not hindered by internal pressures and politics, can be just the type of catalyst you need. A secondary benefit is the interim can share the planning work load, enabling the other team members to have more time during the planning process for their day-to-day duties of running the company.

> *"I consider using an interim manager for those times when objective guidance, unburdened by internal bias, is at a premium. Developing a pricing strategy is a good example."*
> --David Altounian, CEO, iTaggit.com

HANDS-ON COACHING AND TRAINING OF EXISTING STAFF

If you're seeing a need for training in the sales or marketing organization, you can send staff to seminars, hire a professional training company or bring in an interim manager with experience in training and knowledge-transfer.

The decision is easy if you believe your team needs equal parts training and coaching/mentoring. An interim leader with training experience in his discipline can work side-by-side with your staff over a period of time to train and guide.

This chapter looked at seven situations that indicate there's a need for interim or on-demand leadership in sales and marketing. For a growing number of companies, on-demand executives are a smart alternative to permanent hires and consulting firms.

Case Study: Interim Director Product Marketing for Computer and Server Manufacturer

Situation: Engineering was nearing the end of the design and prototype stage for a new line of servers. None of the traditional product marketing work had been done; therefore a timely and successful market introduction was in jeopardy. The company's lean marketing department was completely preoccupied with driving awareness and lead generation campaigns for the company's primary product line.

Solution: The Company's executive management team decided to bring in an interim to prepare the new server line for market introduction until a full-time product manager could be hired.

Result: For a three-month engagement, the interim was on-site four days a week. The interim drove the product launch preparation by forming and leading a launch team consisting of sales, marketing, engineering and operations. During the engagement, the interim conducted primary research to identify the ideal value proposition and assess potential adoption rates, conducted a thorough competitive analysis, kicked off a beta program, developed a positioning and messaging framework, and created a product roadmap. The interim also developed several financial models that linked revenue targets with the required lead generation activities and marketing investment level. When the interim's engagement ended, the company was in position to introduce the product line on schedule and take orders at a major industry trade show.

2.

ON-DEMAND LEADERSHIP IN THE SMALL OR EARLY-STAGE ORGANIZATION

By Paul Travis

"In the big picture, interim leadership is not a premium – you actually pay less. There is cost savings because, if you hire the right people, you can actually get more value for less money than you'd pay if you hired them as an FTE. I think that individuals who are committed to the interim business model (as opposed to those who are really looking to find a permanent job) will likely be able to generate synergy between their various assignments and their relationship networks, thereby delivering higher cumulative value for all parties."
--Brad Furber, President, Xeriton Corporation

Whether in the form of marketing, product management, sales, business development or corporate development, in today's business climate, interim management that drives revenue can apply to every organization. (See Chapter 6 for exceptions).

For the purposes of this book, we delineate the spectrum of organizations into:

➢ small/early stage companies
➢ large/established companies

Though there are many established companies which are small, these breakdowns were chosen primarily because they highlight *the availability of resources.*

In the late 1990's, a book and movie by the name "The Perfect Storm" highlighted all the things that can go wrong at sea, making life treacherous. By contrast, there is a "perfect case" for interim management in startups, given a confluence of factors:

1. Generalists vs. Specialists
2. Limited capital and unlimited demands for expertise
3. Even faster dynamics in the startup marketplace
4. The tug: time to market, sales growth, and control

GENERALISTS vs. SPECIALISTS

As an overgeneralization, companies begin and follow **either** of the following evolutionary paths:

Start With	Team Growth
A general idea or perception of an underserved market	Specific subject matter expertise and history taking a product/service to market
A specific "twist" on a product/service	A more generalized team, to round out the infrastructure and business plan

Regardless of your organization's legacy, you will need generalists as well as specialists. The issue is matching skills set to the organization's need at the time.

> "...companies in very early stage tend to look for people possessing many skills. Of course these generalists are typically masters of none of the particular skills. Soon, these companies grow to require greater strength in a skill area and the existing person often falls short. Though the need for a permanent person with the right skill set is there, the money isn't."
> --Rick Krause, CEO, Boxx Technologies

Let's hypothesize in the realm of legal representation. For your next startup, after finding someone you can afford and giving them a sweet equity package, you hire general counsel on a W2 basis and then ask them to do **everything**

➤ intellectual property

- corporate
- contracts
- corporate securities
- employment
- disability
- personal injury
- immigration
- property/real estate
- energy/environment
- tax
- litigation

Though we must go to war with the army we have, that's quite a battle to send one generalist into.

Same thing is true in on the revenue generation side of the house. You get better results in the capable hands of experts who have deep knowledge within their specialty. This expertise may take the form of:

- sales compensation planning
- distribution channel development/management
- strategic partnerships
- inside and outside sales management
- market research
- international market assessment/entry
- product positioning
- brand management
- customer experience
- product marketing
- corporate communications
- CRM (customer relationship management)
- new media
- social networking

"Early-stage companies go through phases faster than established companies, with each phase typically having different management requirements."
--David Altounian, CEO, iTaggit.com

For example, as this book goes to press, I am on an interim engagement developing the Go-To-Market strategy for a new facet of a $20 million technology company **which already has** a VP of Marketing. This is a CEO who considers the big picture and would rather see results than burn his lieutenant out, much like allocating another locomotive for a sizeable freight train.

My challenge? Create success and demonstrate value-add by driving maximum near-term revenue to offset or even negate the cost of my engagement. The business case is clear.

Consider the abstract idea of sales and marketing leadership as a four-seat VW Beetle -- each seat accommodating a half-time interim for 6 months, filled based on the needs of the organization in its cycle of development.

Can't see going all the way, replacing your permanent players? Then at least envision how to incorporate interims appropriately, as the opportunity arises for your organization.

All the while, you let the organization know that the interim brings industry best-practices and that you expect your staff to make a point of learning from them. On-Demand Leaders are comfortable sharing and teaching, as part of the eventual transition process. They don't perceive their power diminishing by helping others grow.

LIMITED CAPITAL AND UNLIMITED DEMANDS FOR EXPERTISE

It is the rare start-up company that is not bedeviled by very thin capital budgets but infinite demands for high-level expertise. Hiring interim talent gives an early stage company the access they need on a variable-cost basis.

> *"There was no way I could afford to hire someone permanently at that level, (but by tapping into an interim firm) it was a windfall of knowledge for a very reasonable price. It was a perfect fit."*
> --Jim Grogan, CEO, Loreto Bay Development Company

In the world of start-ups and small companies, having access to the depth, breadth and scope of an interim's expertise, without having to hire someone full-time, is a big plus.

EVEN FASTER MARKETPLACE DYNAMICS FOR STARTUPS

When I left Microsoft in the early 90's for a 10-person startup, I remember having the vivid impression that I had "disembarked" an ocean liner and boarded a canoe. Even though I'd been in small companies early on, this stark contrast made it easy to see "big waves" which were virtually imperceptible in a 5,000+ employee company. Readers with a Fortune 1000 background may assume things happen "automatically" in another department or building -- when they actually require bandwidth from someone in the startup, necessarily taking away from other things.

Established companies have rhythms and programs; they have culture and procedure. It is rare to change direction of the "ocean liner" to a great degree. (One of the few standouts is Bill Gates' 1995 call from the helm for Microsoft to make a hard left and embrace the Internet. Industry observers say the company could have been another Polaroid had it not changed direction significantly.)

Startups **constantly** have their ear to the ground to continue seeking out the most opportune and defendable market position – and are thus regularly changing course. In fact, large companies feed off this innovation and acquire these small companies.

In its first year of life, a startup's strategy may be direct-to-consumer and the next year it may embrace the channel. Or, it begins life as a consumer product company and then realizes there is a better fit selling as an original equipment manufacturer (OEM) (). Granted, most permanent leaders could "ride" the shift, but rarely "take charge" like you need. The rolodexes can differ dramatically.

> *"You have the desire to go after the low-hanging fruit first. But because the sky's the limit and you're going for the fences, you see low-hanging fruit everywhere! This happens to everyone, including seasoned executives. The second issue is sweat equity and payment. The common struggle with entrepreneurs is to save money, because they tend to believe that's the only liquid resource they have. The tradeoff is equity, which affects their control (whether they think of ownership or not). These two*
>
> *conditions make it difficult to engage the right kind of seasoned talent long-term to guide the company all the way."*
> --Dr. William Sequeira, former COO, ACD Systems

Having been an investor, officer, founder and consultant in dozens of startups since the early nineties, I've felt this tradeoff. It's ingrained in the startup world:

efficiently serving the market vs. scaling revenues and increasing the capacity of the sales organization vs. retaining equity.

THE TUG: TIME TO MARKET, SALES GROWTH, AND CONTROL

These thoughts are not intended to be a deep dive into the startup success, but a brief word to aid those who haven't yet been down this path. These three factors race in parallel and are critical to the venture's success:

> ➢ The time window for going to market, recouping your investment and generating a profit is short -- and the competition is facing this as well.
>
> ➢ Stagnant sales means the venture can't afford to invest in the infrastructure to take the organization to the next level; worse, it won't be taken seriously in the capital markets for the next round. Rising expenses push the same lever.
>
> ➢ Giving away too much stock in the early phase to management team members can (a) increase long-term dependence on them and hinder your ability to objectively re-evaluate resources, and (b) prematurely dilute.

It would be an overstatement to say that accounting standards today are forcing founders and entrepreneurs to value equity on a cash basis, but things *are* slowly changing.

Savvy interims will accept equity as part of their compensation; this is an individual preference. **You** will want to determine the kind of contribution an interim can make before allowing them to own shares in your corporation or units in your LLC.

> *"You need **professionals**. The company needs someone who has done that before, someone who has worked with larger customers, someone who has built structures that your current VP's have not built; someone who has that experience. The kind of customers you're going to engage, Fortune 100 or 500, these are not people that their current team is engaging. This is a new breed of customer. They're not going to get to the next level with what they've got.*

Traditional entrepreneurs bring a VP in, give them 5% of their company and then wait a year or two for it all to come together. Then, they sit down with their Series A investors who say, 'You've got to go hire an exec - I know a guy'. Then they start with someone new, having already given away 5%!"
--Dr. William Sequeira, former COO, ACD Systems

The on-demand leadership model lets you spread that "concentration" of equity appropriately as the picture becomes clearer over time. Consider a situation where you engage an interim to deliver on specific objectives over 6 or 12 months, including ½ percent in equity with a bonus warrant of another ½ percent, based on certain success criteria. (Compensation is thoroughly discussed in Chapter 10.

IT'S NOT THE VEHICLE; IT'S HOW YOU PILOT

We suggest that the critical success factor in startups is not simply time, money, or talent -- but the **manner in which you engage them**.

We needn't prove that interim management yields a particular percentage-point improvement. All we need do is make the case: in two parallel worlds, the early stage organization that creates more results from the same resources **wins**.

On an advisory board a few years back, I heard a CEO talk about research in his military days, showing that a fighter pilot's success was linked not to his/her dexterity, eyesight or any other physical attribute -- but to the speed in which he/she regularly made decisions and acted upon them.

Think of interims as special "accessories" for your fighter jet, utilized on demand. They provide the ability to execute new initiatives professionally, generating results while leaving infrastructure for someone else to come in and manage when they're gone.

*"You want someone who is bold enough to propose the right solutions! Interims with expertise take pride in launching the new thing, whereas employees look at promotions and job security. A startup needs **subject matter expertise** as well as **structure** (discipline, program management). Interims get to the point, and bring you creativity."*
--Alfred den Besten, former Director of Marketing, Avaya Western Europe

In conclusion, the issues we've discussed -- generalists vs. specialists, faster dynamics for startups, time-to-market, sales growth and control -- are suggestive of opportunities for improvement. The question is whether you or your contemporaries will use them first.

Case Study: Interim VP Marketing for Consumer-Web Start-up

Situation: An early-stage company with four founders and three employees was developing a consumer-based Web site to address a large and fragmented market. As the launch date of the site neared the company had no dedicated marketing resource and limited funding prevented recruiting a full-time executive for the role.

Solution: The CEO brought on an interim head of marketing to orchestrate the launch of the website and build a marketing department.

Results: For four months, the interim conducted key product marketing functions such as a competitive analysis, segmentation, pricing strategy and feature enhancement justifications. He created job descriptions and recruited marketing department personnel. Additionally, in preparation for launch, he created a marketing brief that served as the blueprint for the public relations, advertising, and search marketing and social marketing elements of the launch. Importantly, this work included creating financial models that set the Board's proper expectation levels for subscription growth rate and marketing spend. When the engagement ended, the Web company's soft launch was underway and initial results were tracking to plan

---

3.

ON-DEMAND LEADERSHIP IN THE LARGE ORGANIZATION

By Charles Besondy

There is a common theme that weaves throughout the chapters of this book: how revenue growth - for companies big and small - is directly related to how well-matched the sales and marketing leaders are to the characteristics of the marketplace *at any given point* in time. If markets never changed, or changed very slowly, the leaders responsible for revenue would be able to adapt with the market. However, markets today are hyper-dynamic and staying abreast of change is a critical success factor to all organizations, regardless of size.

So how does this play out for the large organization? What about the company that has scores of sales and marketing leaders; hundreds of product lines and markets around the world?

Large companies are constantly challenged to find the right organizational structure to foster innovation, achieve competitiveness and create customers. The strategic use of on-demand leaders (interim managers) in sales and marketing gives large, highly-structured companies a means to be nimble and quick.

> *"If senior management were honest, they would admit the requirement for an individual with unique expertise in sales or marketing is temporary, whether that means two months or two years. If they were honest, they'd acknowledge the need is short-lived; it's not a career post."*
> --Rick Krause, CEO, Boxx Technologies

OPPORTUNITIES FOR ALTERNATIVE LEADERSHIP

The authors and editor of this book have worked for and consulted with some of the most well-known large-cap companies in the U.S. Our experience in companies such as Microsoft, Paccar, Citigroup, Boeing, Weyerhaeuser, McKesson and Quest Diagnostics has enabled us to see the characteristics of large companies that make these organizations excellent candidates for strategically applying interim managers in sales and marketing.

It's not necessary here to be precise with our definition of "large". Wall Street categorizes organizations based on market capitalization:

- ➤ Large-cap: at least $5 billion
- ➤ Mid-cap: $1-$5 billion
- ➤ Small-cap: $250 million to $1 billion
- ➤ Micro-cap: less than $250 million

However, for the purposes of this chapter we're discussing public and private companies with *annual revenues* of $250 million or higher. It is at this size where the following characteristics become most apparent, but certainly smaller companies can experience some of the same issues.

Here are five characteristics of large organizations that create opportunities for the adoption of interim management:

1. Multiple layers of management
2. Matrix teams
3. Vast products and markets
4. Managers as well-rounded generalists
5. Frequent re-organizations

MULTIPLE LAYERS OF MANAGEMENT

At the risk of sounding trite, the more managers a company has (directors, VP's, Senior VP's, etc) the higher the incidence of transition. A $1B company can easily have scores of VP's and Directors in its sales and marketing departments. At any given time there are going to be multiple vacancies caused by leave of absence, termination, retirement, promotion, re-assignment, etc.

A management team has difficulty operating as a finely-tuned machine when there are cogs missing in the gears. If you doubt this, just take a look at your company's organization chart. How many boxes in sales and marketing are vacant or marked TBH (To Be Hired)? The chart represents just one point in time, so think about over the past 12 months, or dig up the previous charts. You'll be surprised to see that during a 12-month period many key positions, important cogs in the revenue gears of your company, were missing - many for months on end.

> *"Interim management [in large companies] is mostly for gap coverage, or experimenting with a new skill set."*
> --William Leake, CEO, Apogee Search

For each of the empty boxes on the chart, the company could have elected to engage an interim leader rather than "make do" until a permanent executive could be found and hired.

MATRIX TEAMS

Ask any sales or marketing leader within a large company how many project teams they are on and the number may surprise you. Most of an executive's day can be spent participating on planning teams, strategic teams, product teams, productivity teams, even teams planning the move to a new facility. That's life in a large company.

Consider the make-up of these teams. Most, if not all, are temporary. They were formed to address an issue or accomplish an initiative. The teams may be relatively short-lived, or can span a year or two, as with a product team. The point is: they're temporary.

The other aspect of teams in today's large company is they are comprised of people from different departments, different facilities and often different countries. The team is assembled in order to have the right combination of folks to achieve the goal.

Inside of this structure gaps can exist. The person with the right marketing skills or background for the team's project may not be available, or may not exist at all. The individual with global sales compensation expertise may be on sabbatical and unavailable for the team.

Interim managers are ideal solutions to round out project teams. The short-term project has defined goals and parameters and has been formed to really focus brain-power on a *specific* problem or opportunity. What a perfect environment for interim marketing and sales leaders!

> *"Established companies frequently face situations where it makes no sense to staff up for a one-time major event, such as a product launch. Bringing in interims to manage major elements of the launch and then go away is very appealing."*
> --David Altounian, CEO, iTaggit.com

NUMEROUS PRODUCT LINES AND MARKETS

A large corporation today is really a very large collection of brands and products sold into a dizzying number of market segments.

Each product lives or dies based on how well it generates profit while satisfying the customer better than its competitors. This wouldn't be such a formidable task if: the customer's needs weren't constantly evolving, competitors weren't continually changing strategies, new technologies weren't frequently disrupting or threatening the product category, and geopolitical forces weren't routinely impacting the supply chain.

This situation puts incredible pressure on the organization to have in place marketing and sales leaders for each product who think and act one step ahead of their customers and competitors. It requires leaders who are unbiased and very, very current.

It's okay to remember "what worked" last year and the year before. However, it's very risky to rely 100% on those same strategies and tactics *this* year because the product exists in a completely different world than it did 12 or 24 months ago.

Interim managers in marketing or sales can function as the experts in the "now". They can provide critical insight to product teams who are heavily influenced (and biased) by the past. Unlike consultants who might provide a futuristic perspective, interims are in the office, doing the work. Even a temporary infusion of current skills and knowledge can make a difference in the longevity of a product or brand.

There's another reason sales and marketing interims should be widely used in large companies. The work-load associated with supporting a product varies depending on where the product is in its lifecycle. Typically, for marketing and sales, the few months prior to a product launch and the two months after launch are the busiest. If you're in retail, holidays or grand opening events are particularly crazy for you.

Interims give companies the flexibility to staff up during peak times.

Large companies are more likely than small companies to service a variety of market segments and to have a global perspective to their sales and marketing efforts.

The use of interim management in Europe and the U.K. is very common and the talent pool is wide and deep. Companies with facilities outside the U.S. would be wise not turn a cold shoulder to these alternative resources. Indeed, for some companies without established global brands (and the reputation that accompanies the brand), the use of just-in-time managers can enable a U.S. company to quickly set up shop in other countries compared to recruiting local managers to join a "foreign" company.

Therefore, because of the sheer volume of products and markets addressed by a large company, the opportunities for leveraging interim talent in the large organization are significant.

MANAGERS AS WELL-ROUNDED GENERALISTS

Large companies believe in having succession plans and management development programs. Typically, a manager will be identified as having potential "for upper management" and that person is groomed and mentored for years. We all know companies who have policies of moving executives from department to department, country to country, in an effort to prepare them for a senior management role. The goal is that senior managers should be well-rounded individuals with broad knowledge of the business.

So, a newly-promoted CMO very likely had stints as a product manager, regional sales manager, head of research, maybe even spent some time in field operations.

We're certainly not taking issue with this practice. Top executives need to know how the organization works, and they need to have form solid relationships throughout the company.

What we wish to point out is: the grooming process tends to make generalists out of specialists. That's by design, you say. You're right. But this process isn't happening to just one person; it's happening to scores or perhaps hundreds of the company's brightest sales and marketing people who are in development programs being groomed for bigger and better things.

So, the question is this. If the company's brightest sales and marketing people are being "generalized" in management prep programs, who's providing the innovation and leadership in specialized areas?

Let's say John is in the company's management grooming program. He is transferred from VP of Customer Relationship Marketing (CRM), to the U.K., where he will head a sales region. Replacing him is Amy, who was Director of Advertising. For the next several months, Amy is not only going to be learning what it's like to be a VP, but what it means to drive the CRM initiative within the company/brand.

For those several months the performance in the department can be expected to decline while Amy gets up to speed. She was a specialist in advertising. Now she's running CRM. Yes, she has people working for her, but just how innovative can she be early on? She hasn't earned her "specialist stripes" in CRM yet.

Multiply this scenario a dozen times over and you begin to see the potential problem. However, the intelligent use of interim managers can prevent many of the performance declines.

Let's go back to John and Amy for a minute. Imagine the performance gain for Amy if she could engage an interim manager, a highly regarded specialist in CRM, to assist her for a few months. The interim could help her see the strengths and weaknesses of her organization and systems without any bias. The interim could pitch in and help run programs, evaluate new technology, whatever was needed to give Amy time to get up to speed. With the interim's help, not only will Amy find her stride faster, the performance of the department won't suffer due to John's departure.

When management stars are being groomed as generalists, interims can provide the infusion of specialized skills and knowledge.

If one is an ambitious and talented manager, you consider it a plus to join a company that believes in developing its own talent; grooming its managers for promotion, or as some express it, "hiring for a career". However, being employed by a company with this philosophy doesn't guarantee that you'll be immune to attractive job offers from other companies.

It's also possible the jury is still out on whether a "promote from within" strategy saves the company money. Training isn't a zero-cost endeavor. The opportunity cost can be high in situations where the manager in the position is still learning the ropes.

"A lot of interims are seen as extra cost- not as extra knowledge! At Avaya, I did a spin-off. Of all the 3,000 employees, I was the only one who had spin-off knowledge. I can do this in my sleep."
--Alfred den Besten, former Director of Marketing, Avaya Western Europe

FREQUENT RE-ORGANIZATIONS

I have friends who work in large companies. Whenever I visit them they'll have half their office stuff in boxes. It's because they get moved every six months and they've gotten tired of packing and repacking their office. They just keep half the stuff in the boxes now.

In the last large company I worked for, I had six different bosses in four years. Many of you reading this are thinking I was lucky to have just one boss every eight months. Companies are constantly reorganizing themselves-re-shuffling the deck in hopes of finding the ideal level of efficiency and competitiveness.

Then there are the mergers and acquisitions (M&A); many books have been written about the organizational and cultural challenges of M&A events. The relevant point for this discussion is that in any reorganization, merger, or acquisition there are bound to be gaps - gaps that rob a company of momentum and focus.

Sometimes an interim executive is needed to step in and help steer the marketing or sales ship because the existing management team is completely occupied with pre-merger planning.

Nearly every merger is accompanied by layoffs. As marketing departments are coalesced and sales teams realigned, gaps inevitably appear. Perhaps the realignment of the sales regions left one region without a VP temporarily. Or, the person slotted for the VP of Marketing spot in the new company decided at the last minute he didn't want to relocate.

In times of transition, gaps emerge. On-demand leaders in sales and marketing can fill those gaps so that momentum is never lost.

INTERIMS AND REGULATION COMPLIANCE

Companies can find it awkward to explain turnover in top sales or marketing positions. For public companies, it's more serious, thanks to Sarbanes Oxley[1] and the "material event" requirement that a company must make public information which might impact a company's stability or performance. Section 409 of the Act is just ambiguous enough that a vacancy in a top marketing or sales position

---

SNAPSHOT

"We got very concrete results from the interim marketing leader we engaged for 12-18 months:

1. He was able to see the value proposition in a way that was not there before, and did some brand architecture work that really helped everyone be on the same page.

2. He transferred that architecture into outbound communications, in particular getting us PR and engaging key trade magazines to talk about the product, as well as ancillary publications that positioned the product where it needed to be.

3. Additional work was done in market research – so the marketing department was able to further influence both sales, in terms of how to engage prospects, as well as product development, in terms of shaping usability

4. Because of his experience and objectivity, we were able, for the first time, to quantify the market size of the opportunity for this particular product. It affected our perception of the lifetime value of the customer and our future investments into customer acquisition."

---

[1] Section 409 of Sarbanes Oxley requires public companies to disclose "on a rapid and current basis" material information regarding changes in a company's financial condition or operations as we, by rule, determine to be necessary or useful for the protection of investors and in the public interest.

could require disclosure, depending on counsel from your Compliance Officer.

Public companies faced with frequent turnover in these roles, or faced with the prospect of a lengthy vacancy, should consider the use of interim executives to fill these critical gaps. First and foremost, the interim will be getting the job done during the engagement. Secondly, the fact that the individuals are interim managers and not FTE's *may* not need to be reported as such to be compliant with Sarbanes Oxley. (Confer with your legal and compliance advisors on this matter).

The company has a qualified executive performing as the top sales or marketing leader, even as a search progresses for a full-time individual. The risk to company performance is mitigated.

In the opinion of one of our subject matter experts:

> *"If you look at NASDAQ or TSX in Canada, there are regulations as to making disclosures about bringing in officers and senior executives. So when you hire someone and they don't work out, you let them go, and then you hire someone else, and they don't work out, so they're gone too. Eventually analysts start to catch up and start writing about what's going on – which has a negative effect on share price. So an undervalued benefit of hiring an interim is that you preserve your reputation, your credibility. Basically going the interim route frees you of having your laundry out in front of everybody."*
> --Dr. William Sequeira, former COO, ACD Systems

By nature of their size and complexity, large companies have a perpetual need for on-demand leadership in sales and marketing functions. Forward-thinking organizations will form alliances with leading interim providers in order to have a ready source of just-in-time executives.

4.

BRIDGING GAPS DURING THE SEARCH FOR A PERMANENT HIRE

By Paul Travis

"I would not be opposed to bringing in interim management if I knew the recruitment process would drag on for months."
--Rick Krause, CEO, Boxx Technologies

In considering the notion of bridging the FTE-hiring gap, we'll look -- over the next few chapters -- at the questions of **whether, when, how,** and **when not to** engage interim marketing/sales leadership.

Begin by asking yourself these three questions:

1. How long do you anticipate it will take to complete your search for a senior leader or contributor to your team -- from identification of needs to first day of contribution?
2. What are the costs:
   a. Intangible costs to you and/or other staffers of having to "carry the load" while the seat remains empty?
   b. Opportunity cost of being without a dedicated individual driving key sales and marketing initiatives?

3. Given the increasing rate of change in the business world, how much are you willing to bet:
   a. That the chosen candidate will work out long term?
   b. That you won't end up fulfilling a severance package?
   c. That the needs of your enterprise (when he/she starts) will be the same as when you wrote the job description?

HOW LONG DOES A DIRECTOR, VP OR C-LEVEL SEARCH TAKE?

If you believe the search to be a 4 – 6 week process for your organization, then any investment in "bridging the gap" is likely to be an unnecessary distraction from the key objective of reeling in said talent.

Our group of subject matter experts was split: half believed that such management searches take 3 to 6 months; the other half say that they take 6 to 9 months to complete.

Pricing of products and services have varying levels of elasticity. So do certain raw materials. But human resources rarely do.

You and your staff can only take on so many extra slices of senior level "secondary" work atop a full plate of primary work for so long. Sooner or later, "carrying the load" while the seat remains empty will take its toll:

➢ Stress on your people and/or their families
➢ Distraction from primary work
➢ Diminishing quality of primary and/or secondary work

Of course, the bigger question of what your sales or marketing initiatives **could** have done, had there been a dedicated individual in place, will change with every situation. Every organization and point in time is unique. In this case, your mileage truly will vary.

We can at least do some cross-industry projection. If the typical company requires gross revenue of 5-10x the individual's pay level for net profit to cover his or her pay, and the average marketing or sales exec is drawing $200,000 annually, then by gross estimates the baseline lost revenue of that seat remaining empty for 6 months is $750,000 -- and probably much more.

In order to truly model the answer for your organization, you are likely to require the services of an outsider to perform this analysis with objectivity. And this brings up another potential issue:

> *"When a company enters transition mode, there is housekeeping necessary before the company can go all the way. Once that housekeeping is done, sometimes it becomes evident that the situation is different than what it was before. Now the problem appears. Most CEO's and COO's, when they identify the problem, they say 'we have to plug the hole' (a defensive rather than a strategic reaction). Rarely, however, do the performance milestones of the contractor include a strategic assessment of the situation **and** they're not given the mandate to develop a 360-degree view, which is critical. You have to allocate cycles for the housekeeping, not just more doing."*
> --Dr. William Sequeira, Former COO, ACD Systems

HOW MUCH ARE YOU WILLING TO BET?

Your first bet is on your selected FTE working out long term. Of execs who don't work out for one reason or another, the minority leave within 12 months. (There is a reason this is a typical headhunter guarantee period!) Many more depart after 12 months.

Second bet: In the United States, though most employment situations are termed "at will" and may be terminated at any time, senior management packages frequently include severance packages up-front which make short-term hires very expensive. In most European countries, it is difficult and costly to get rid of people who are not working out – frequently costing 2 to 3 months pay plus *another month for every year worked.*

The third bet is much bigger – that the business landscape didn't shift on you. Consider:

> *"If you're going to go through the same old time-intensive process, where you write the description and you get HR bringing in recruits and you're going to see if your **left hand** likes him and then you're going to see if your **right hand** likes*

him... by the time you're done with all that, your competition has run 2 circles around you! And what's worse is that, during those 6 months, the market changed on you – and we're not talking minor steps. We're talking about significant changes in competitive landscape where the guy who was well-suited 6 months ago now is very ill-suited and he's going to get kicked by the current circumstances. The amount of time that people spend on the 'fit' – which speaks about emotions, politics, how people get along in relationships – yes it's very important, but it's getting squeezed right now. "
--Dr. William Sequeira, former COO, ACD Systems

Herbert Meyer, in his 2007 global intelligence briefing for CEO's, entitled What In The World Is Going On?, cites one of four major transformations taking place: "The restructuring of American business means we are coming to the end of the age of the employer and employee. With all this fracturing of businesses into different and smaller units, employers can't guarantee jobs anymore because they don't know what their companies will look like next year. Everyone is on their way to becoming an independent contractor."

WHEN TO BRIDGE

One mode of tapping leadership on demand was presented in the Introduction: serially, moving from interim to interim, based on the evolving needs of the organization. Some organizations may find the logic and cost effectiveness enough to change and never look back.

Most leaders, however (and some of our subject matter experts) see interim management as a stop-gap means. Consider this idea:

*"If the goal is to get to market as soon as possible, why take 6 months to go through the hiring process and **then** begin the orientation process when you can actually get done what you need to get done? ... My recommendation is that, every time you change a CMO or a VP of Sales, always use 1 to 6 months of interim to 'break things up'. They get rid of any inheritance. The first thing the new FTE hears is 'how people used to do the job'. The interim cleans up and turns the position over to a new FTE fresh. I believe the new executive will be at least twice as effective. ... In 1-2 months, the interim knows the character and the culture. He or she can create the job description from his diary. "*
--Alfred den Besten, former Director of Marketing, Avaya Western Europe

The suggestion may seem radical but others we interviewed suggested that regularly seeking interim and permanent talent in parallel was a good practice.

THE PARALLEL STAFFING STRATEGY

Consider tapping an interim for a quick strategic sales or marketing audit (usually one month) while HR goes through its process of updating the incumbent's job description and replacing him/her.

The key benefit is new thinking, questioning of old assumptions and strategic planning -- from someone who can work with continuity, rather than a consulting firm which leaves you with a pretty report.

The secondary benefit is to get someone in who can put out the fires and drive initiatives so that the work doesn't fall onto the shoulders of you or others.

A potential third benefit will depend on the individual -- namely to test drive the individual for fit, contribution, etc. Not every interim is interested in a permanent, W2 role. But if the fit is good, many will give it consideration.

Alternatively, you may engage a sales or marketing leader for 6 to 12 months, and then offer "another" interim project so he or she can still derive the variety that often drives this individual -- without actually forcing the W2 question (which can push their buttons).

To the point, the view of the authors is that **everything** today is "interim". It's just a matter of degree.

The final benefit of the Parallel Staffing Strategy is applicable only to public companies. For exchanges such as NASDAQ in the US or TSX in Canada, there are regulations about disclosing changes in officers and senior executives. Repeated changes in a position will catch the eye of analysts, who begin either asking questions or writing speculative commentary -- both of which mean that a problem on the revenue generation side has an unexpected negative impact on share price.

Phrasing this in the positive, the undervalued benefit of interim leadership is preservation and control of reputation, credibility and share price. Choosing the interim route frees you of having to air your laundry publicly in the entire marketplace.

5.

TIPS FOR SCOPING THE ENGAGEMENT

By Charles Besondy

Defining the scope of an interim engagement is the single most important step an executive can take to ensure a successful outcome. This seems such a fundamental and common-sense step that I actually considered removing this chapter from the book. However, I thought back on the scores of scoping conversations I've had and recalled how ill-prepared many of the clients were for the important scoping conversation. The chapter deserves to live.

The engagement scope is a blueprint for the project's formal agreement between the interim leader and your organization. It concisely defines the: *who, what, where, when, why, how, and cost* of the engagement. Most of the burden of documenting the scope should fall on the interim manager, but you, as the party paying the bill, want to think through key points prior to sitting down with the interim to map out the scope.

> *"Be clear on what you're trying to accomplish with the engagement."*
> --Freddie Carroll, Partner, StarTech Early Ventures

DEFINE THE PAIN OR OPPORTUNITY YOU WANT ADDRESSED

Before having a conversation with a potential interim manager, write down the problem you're trying to solve. This gives focus and clarity to the remainder of the scope. Don't be general or high-level here. It's not enough to state, "20% revenue shortfall expected next quarter." Rather, get to the expected root cause of the revenue shortfall. Example: "Our inconsistent delivery of the value proposition, combined with a lack of sales process in the central region, is extending the sales cycle from 3 months to 6 months."

Instead of stating, "We need to fill the gap at VP of Marketing while we search for a permanent hire," look at the opportunity cost of not having a marketing leader in place for 4-6 months. What critical initiatives are being delayed or postponed as a result? What is the ripple effect as another senior executive, or you, take on the additional responsibility? What's the value of your time (and sanity)?

> *"Describe the value first…what is the pain or cost associated with not filling that role?"*
> --William Leake, CEO, Apogee Search

In situations where you aren't sure about the root cause of the problem, it's wise to define a preliminary engagement around a process of discovery combined with a recommendation for action. Once the recommendation is complete, you and the interim can scope a second engagement aimed at implementing the recommendations.

The more precisely you pin a cost to the problem, the easier it will be to justify the investment in an interim engagement. Is $2MM in revenue at risk? Is 1% of market share, valued at $15MM, at risk because the test marketing schedule of a new product is in jeopardy? Are you experiencing delays in acquiring $20MM additional financing because you're spending half your time in the VP Marketing role, rather than 100% of your time in the CEO role? Loss of opportunity and loss of business momentum can have huge ramifications for your organization. Be realistic and honest with yourself about the risks and the costs.

After you've thought through the project yourself, meet with the interim leader to further brainstorm. The scope can be mapped out on anything from a white board to a cocktail napkin; you're not creating a legal document, so don't get hung up on legalese at this point.

> *"Be crisp and clear about…what your expectations are for the end of the job."*
> --Rick Krause, CEO, Boxx Technologies

Below (Figure 4) is a convenient visual aid for the scoping meeting with your interim manager. Draw this diagram on the whiteboard or piece of paper. To the right list the top-3 objectives for the engagement. The horizontal line represents the timeline for the engagement. It will most likely be 3-9 months, but can be any period of time. Above the line, list the key milestones for the engagement, such as deliverables, recommendations, important meetings, etc. Below the timeline, mark dates for key relevant events that will be occurring during the engagement period. These are dates that impact or are impacted by the engagement in some way

Figure 4 helps to provide a framework for the scoping conversation. Once the scoping diagram is complete, with key dates and milestones, you're set to discuss the engagement's requirements in more detail.

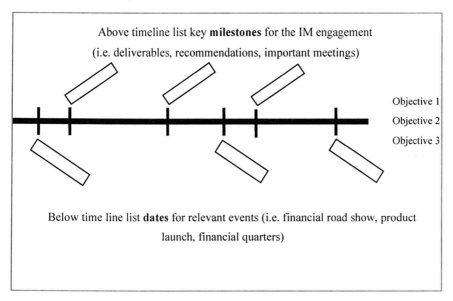

Figure 4: The Scoping Diagram

The remainder of the chapter is devoted to tips and considerations for the scoping process.

1. Collaborate with the interim to define the specifics
2. Set objectives for outcomes, milestones, and deliverables
3. Define the day-to-day responsibilities and parameters
4. Make definitions clear
5. Don't overlook the orientation phase and transition phase
6. Define IT requirements
7. Define compensation

COLLABORATE WITH THE INTERIM LEADER TO DEFINE THE SPECIFICS

Once you have a clear picture of the problem you're trying to solve or the opportunity you're attacking, it's time to sit down with the interim and discuss the parameters. Use the scoping diagram (Figure 4) to provide focus and a framework for the conversation.

This interaction will be an early indication as to whether or not you're talking to the right expert for the job. A seasoned interim manager will know what questions to ask to concisely define the scope. He'll think of points to consider that you overlooked. If he isn't insightful, that should be a warning flag that you're not talking to an experienced interim that has faced these issues before and knows how to address them systematically.

SET OBJECTIVES FOR OUTCOMES, MILESTONES, AND DELIVERABLES

During the scoping conversation with the interim, describe what a successful outcome of the engagement would look like to you. Be as specific as possible. From this vision, the engagement's objectives will be cast. If you haven't already, write the objectives in the scoping diagram (Figure 4) to the right of the timeline. During the scoping conversation with the interim, describe what a successful outcome of the engagement would look like to you. Be as specific as possible. From this vision, the engagement's objectives will be cast. If you haven't already, write the objectives in the scoping diagram (Figure 4) to the right of the timeline.

Objectives must be specific and measurable, or at least observable:

What are the results you expect?
Example:

> ➤ Develop a sales training program for the new product by end of Q2
> ➤ Regional sales managers trained and accredited by end of July
> ➤ New product sales achieve 15% of total sales by end of Q3
> ➤ Implement new commission plan
> ➤ Incorporates all product lines
> ➤ Generates greater focus on most profitable lines

What are the primary deliverables you expect?

41

Example:

- ➢ Sales training manual for instructor
- ➢ Training materials and exam for participants
- ➢ Training manual in Word format
- ➢ Training materials in PowerPoint format
  - o Interim to create the documents
  - o Company's graphic department to provide graphics support and printing
  - o Interim manager will conduct one training class by July 15
  - o Summary report by July 30

What are the key milestones that you want to track?
Example:

- ➢ Review and approve training methodology and outline by June 1
- ➢ Review and approve first draft of training materials by June 15
- ➢ Final approval by June 30
- ➢ Summary report by July 30

DEFINE THE DAY-TO-DAY RESPONSIBILITIES AND PARAMETERS

An interim engagement is typically more complex than a consulting project. The interim manager is usually on site part of every week. He or she generally interacts and collaborates with others in the organization and with the organization's customers and vendors. The interim can also have direct reports. In short, the interim executive functions just like a regular senior manager in the company. In comparison, most consulting projects don't involve the same degree of collaboration, interaction, or on-site presence.

As a result, the scope and description for an interim management engagement have considerations a consulting project may not. It's helpful to think about these considerations as if you were writing a job description for the position the interim is filling. In many cases, a job description already exists because the leader is filling a gap during a transition.

Here are questions to answer during the scoping discussion:

1. What is the management structure above and below the interim 'position?

2. If the interim executive has a staff, what are the expectations for activities such as staff meetings, one-on-ones, annual performance evaluations, etc.

3. What regularly scheduled cross-functional project and team meetings need to be attended?

4. What are the schedules and expectations regarding department meetings, executive staff meetings, or Board meetings?

5. What type of decisions can the interim make, and which decisions must be discussed with you first? In short, what are the limits of authority? (Note: nothing will restrict an interim leader's effectiveness more than for a senior executive to override or second-guess decisions or directives to their team).

6. Setting expectations for the time parameters is especially important. Which days of the week will the interim be on site, and which days will they be off site, but working for you? What hours of the day will be "on the clock"? Are weekends considered an extension of the work week, or not? Of course, the engagement start date and end date have to be clearly understood by both parties. Learn if the interim can be flexible if required. For instance, must the engagement always be Monday – Wednesday because he or she has another assignment that occupies Thursday and Friday?

7. The interim should be required to keep a record of the actual days worked.

MAKE DEFINITIONS CLEAR

The engagement scope and formal agreement must include definitions of key terms. Your definitions can vary, but here are a few important terms to consider. (Your attorney may have other ideas, but I've found these terms and definitions to be useful and readily understood).

1. Engagement period: this is the number of total calendar days in the engagement from start to finish.

2. Total work days: this is the total number of days that will be worked within the engagement period. This is a very important number because

in most cases the interim manager's fee is based on the number of days worked multiplied by a day-rate.

3. Work days: What days of the week will be worked? Which days will be on-site, which days off-site? A work day consists of how many hours? What hours each day will be worked? Be specific, is it required that the interim be there at 7 AM or is 9 AM okay? When does a work day end? At 6 PM, or whenever the work is done?

4. Off days: What, if any, days each week is the interim not working for you? Also, there may be days during the engagement that the executive will be unavailable due to previous commitments, or vacation. Those dates need to be listed in the scope and agreement.

5. Exchange days: This term can refer to a day that is treated differently in order to keep the day-count in line with total estimate. For instance, I might "take off" a normal work day because of a previous unscheduled day on which I had to work. Typically, if I work unexpectedly on a Saturday, I'll arrange to take an extra day off the following week. Or, if something unexpected comes up and I'm unavailable to work on a scheduled work day, I'll work an extra day within the next week as a make-up. Finally, ask your interim what his policy is regarding weekend work, or work that exceeds a certain number of hours a day.

DON'T OVERLOOK THE ORIENTATION PHASE AND TRANSITION PHASE

How an interim engagement is started and finished has a lot to do with its success. When scoping a project, discuss openly how the interim and the engagement will be socialized within the organization (Chapter 7 covers socialization); what orientation they require and what actions or deliverables are required at the end of the project to ensure a smooth transition.

The orientation phase can be simple and quick, or more complex. Here are some questions to consider together with the interim:

1. What product demonstrations or product training classes are required?
2. What existing plans, documents and research need to be read?
3. What facilities or events need to be visited?
4. What vendors need to be met?
5. What people within the organization need to be met first?

The transition phase leading up to the project's conclusion can have special requirements. Discuss these questions with the interim:

1. Is a permanent hire going to replace the interim at the end of the engagement? If so, what can be done to ensure a smooth transition?
2. If vendors and other 3rd parties are going to be involved, how is the management of these relationships going to be transferred or terminated?
3. If plans and recommendations are being developed during the engagement, how is ownership of the plans going to be transferred, and to whom?
4. Will the executive be available to answer questions after the engagement is over?

DEFINE IT REQUIREMENTS

It's easy to take IT support for granted these days. Many executives, when hiring an employee, are accustomed to simply signing an IT request form and a PC, phone, cell phone, and user guides for the intranet, etc. will be waiting for the new employee on the first day.

This level of support may or may not be appropriate for the interim engagement, therefore, discuss it during the scoping conversation.

Will a computer be provided by the company, or will the interim need to bring a notebook PC to the office each day? (Check with your IT manager to see what security regulations must be followed).

1. Will the interim's PC have access to network printers and fax machines?
2. The interim will need to have a company email address and access to the email server.
3. Will the interim have a desk or office?
4. Will the interim require an office phone, or company-supplied cell phone, or pager?
5. Will the interim require security privileges to access the company intranet?
6. Will the interim require a security badge for access to the building?
7. If the interim will be traveling for your company, can they use the services of the company's travel department, or do they book their own travel?

DEFINE COMPENSATION AND PAYMENT PERIODS

Chapter 10 deals with compensation, so it won't be discussed in detail here. During the scoping conversation, the interim won't be able to give you an accurate estimate because she'll need time to consider all the factors that have arisen in the scoping conversation that impact the work she'll be doing and the time it will require.

Most interim executive's fees are based on a day-rate. The fee quoted will likely be a total price for the engagement, but calculated based on the number of days to be worked.

The day-rate may vary depending on the duration of the project and type of work being done. Don't be surprised if short engagements have higher day-rates than longer engagements of three or more months. Furthermore, you can expect that an engagement with a high value-add factor will have higher day-rates than lower-value, tactical engagements.

You and the interim should discuss if it makes sense for both parties to consider deferring a portion of the fees and awarding the deferred portion if certain objectives are achieved. See Chapter 10 for information about structuring deferred compensation into an interim engagement.

By following these guidelines, you and the interim leader will go a long ways toward accurately scoping the requirements and parameters of the engagement.

6.

WHEN NOT TO USE AN ON-DEMAND LEADER

By Paul Travis

This book makes a significant case for the use of leadership on demand. The two cases when it would be ill advised are:

1. When the culture is completely "against" it, and the interim leader would immediately be set up for failure
2. When your board or management prefers a written assessment from a top-tier consulting company over an individual rolling up his or her sleeves and solving the problem(s) at hand.

CULTURAL FIT

A few years ago, I reconnected by email with a CEO of a $250 million company. When I mentioned that I'd gone from independent (or "single shingle") consulting to being a partner in an Interim Firm, he replied: *"we don't use external resources"*.

Regardless of the value of the objectivity and style a new leader would bring to "shake things up"; an interim may not be welcome if your culture is indeed so tight-laced. There are already enough challenges for an interim.

> *"If you're an interim, your staff looks at you just like the child looks at the stepfather: 'You're not my daddy'. ... When you confront the party line, the 'them' is going to attack the 'us'. It is sometimes overtly, but mostly in very subtle ways, such as not cooperating, not providing data to the interim, etc."*
> --Dr. William Sequeira, former COO, ACD Systems

In this era of outsourcing and ultra-competitive pressure from home and abroad, few companies can afford to be so narrow-minded over the long term. In reality, your competitors **are** changing with the times, so you may be moving backwards without even trying!

MCKINSEYITIS

If your board or management team members were groomed at Fortune 500 companies, they are likely to believe that solving problems requires a team from Deloitte, Bain, McKinsey, et al. The fear always looms of getting fired for making a bad decision, so paying six figures for a thorough report that sits on the desk (or worse, the bookshelf) will certainly be reassuring.

From a skeptic's perspective, the notion that you would bring in a "transient", entrust them with your people, and give the authority to make decisions – no matter how far they roll up their sleeves – is probably just too far of a stretch for individuals with such backgrounds.

As a mentor taught me, "We're mostly *down* on what we're not *up* on."

Humans are creatures of habit, and we tend to repeat patterns. Whether the boy follows the footsteps of his father, or does everything differently, his focus is always energetically on the dad. Change in focus only occurs as he seeks out **other** examples and role models – sometimes by meeting other people, other times by reading about new ways of operating.

YOU MUST BE CLEAR AN INTERIM LEADER IS WHAT YOU WANT

> *"When I need someone to fill a gap, my first tendency is to talk to other CEO's and see if they know of anyone available for a temporary period of time. In the past, I wouldn't have thought of calling an interim provider firm because I have never considered looking for or retaining an 'interim manager'. What I was really doing was considering using an expert for a set period of time. The term "interim manager" wasn't in my mind, and frankly, I think I would have had a hard time selling my Board on the idea of retaining an interim VP of Marketing. There can be a stigma to the term; it sounds like you're trying to patch a problem rather than solve a problem. This, in my mind, is a marketing challenge for folks who are interim managers.*
>
> *For me, this is about semantics and perception, because I have successfully used managers and executives in interim roles. I*

*never set out to solve the problem with an 'interim manager',
even though that's what I did in the end."*
--David Altounian, CEO, iTaggit.com

When your staff, your board, and peers from outside ask you why you chose to bring in a "temporary" executive, you can say with a clear conscience: for the same reason I hire a lawyer by the hour and pay my mechanic to work on my car by the visit. I don't want to hire them for a whole year!

One of the best ways to reinforce this belief is to learn what has worked for your peers. Ask friends for interim leaders they've worked with and interview them. Check your gut as you listen to them – does it ring true? Do you trust this person enough to trust them with a department or division of your company? Remember, the beautiful thing about interims is that there is no long-term commitment. In life, the purpose of going out on a first date is to see if you want a second date. Give him or her a project that is **not** your highest priority, and let him or her prove the value.

Also, the very fact you're reading this book is exposing you to the **kind** of results one can expect. (See Chapters 1, 2, 3, 9 and 10 for Case Studies and "Snapshots" of success).

7.

SOCIALIZING THE ENGAGEMENT

By Charles Besondy

Next to properly defining the scope of an engagement, nothing contributes to the success of an interim assignment more than properly socializing it throughout the organization.

Explaining the interim's role to the organization is usually the responsibility of the CEO or other senior executive, such as the COO. All constituents must be considered for socializing:

1. The Board
2. Peer-level executives
3. Department staff members
4. Cross-functional work teams
5. Key vendors or partners
6. Important customers

PAVING THE WAY WITH THE BOARD

Depending on the size of the company and the position to be filled, the CEO or COO will inform the Board of the intention to solve a particular problem or address a specific opportunity with an interim executive. There must be clarity at the Board level on the issue; otherwise support for the decision will be on shaky ground.

It's a good idea to share with the Board the thought process and alternative solutions that were considered. It's equally important to communicate the cost of not doing anything. For additional tips on considerations in compensating the interim leader, refer to Chapter 10.

"The way I've done it before is first make sure that the CEO and Board are in full understanding of what the issue is. If there's no clarity on the issue, there's no point in proceeding."
--Dr. William Sequeira, former COO, ACD Systems

THE INTERIM MANAGER'S PEER GROUP

Always involve the management team in the decision-making process and establish a level of understanding *prior* to engaging with an interim leader. If you're filling a senior executive role discuss it with the other senior management members. If the interim is filling a director-level role, make sure the other department directors are on board with the situation and the decision.

The CEO should look to the top HR executive for assistance with socializing the interim engagement within the organization.

The company's management team could express concerns—implicitly or explicitly—as to how loyal and gung-ho the interim will be compared to them. This attitude can be present in management teams that have worked together for some time and where large individual incentives are in place for company performance. You can ease their minds by emphasizing that the interim leader's objectives are aligned with the management team's objectives. If the engagement's fee has a portion that is deferred, based on results, this fact should be mentioned.

"What I'd want other execs to know is that role clarification and interplay with other company resources is critical."
--Brad Furber, President, Xeriton Corporation

It can't hurt to also review with the management team that the interim has signed all the necessary non-disclosure agreements and can be trusted as much as any employee.

THE INTERIM MANAGER'S DEPARTMENT

This requires skillful communication and sensitivity. It's not enough to just distribute an e-mail on the day the interim starts. Instead, days before the interim manager is set to start, the executive making the announcement should conduct an in-person meeting with the interim's direct reports and others in the department if size permits.

If relevant, acknowledge everyone for their extra hard work and accomplishments while filling the gap. Odds are high that people on the team have been under a lot of stress and you need to recognize the additional hours and sacrifices. At the same time, avoid suggesting that their hard work failed to make a difference. Some of the team may see your decision to bring in an interim as a reflection on their inability to pick up the slack. This will create a sense of anxiety in the team that could lead to resentment toward the interim leader.

Here are some tips for "breaking the news" to the interim's department:

1. Review the business situation that led to the interim engagement decision. This includes a discussion of the engagement's objectives. It's important the team understand the big picture and what's at stake.
2. Review the interim's bio and past achievements to establish his/her credibility with the team.
3. Review the interim's level of authority. In most cases they should be seen as being no different than a new permanent executive coming on board. If they will be conducting performance reviews at some point during the engagement, this should be mentioned. (On the first day of the engagement it is wise to review again the authority guidelines with the team and the interim together).
4. Review the time frame of the engagement, including days they will be on site, etc. Depending on the situation, you may wish to emphasize that the engagement is indeed a temporary one. You should be up-front with your plans to eventually fill the position with a permanent hire, or not. If you and the interim are approaching this engagement as "try before you buy" it's best to disclose this fact to the team.
5. Answer questions.

THE CROSS-FUNCTIONAL WORK TEAMS

An interim sales or marketing executive is not going to operate in a silo (at least we hope not). In marketing for example the interim and his team could participate in any number of project teams. The following list of cross-functional teams is not uncommon for a marketing manager in a mid-tier company:

1. Product A launch team
2. Product B market requirements team

3. Marketing process team
4. Lead generation and qualification task force
5. CRM system implementation team
6. Agency review team
7. Market segmentation and sizing team
8. Global branding team
9. Annual shareholder meeting team
10. Annual sales meeting team

The point is these teams can have high-level management members from Engineering, Manufacturing, HR, Operations, Legal, and IT departments. Furthermore, the team members can be spread around the globe. All need to know that an interim leader is coming on board to work with them.

A busy CEO can't take the time to communicate with each project team, but he can certainly request that someone in the interim's department make the announcements prior to them coming on board.

VENDORS AND PARTNERS

Socialization can't be limited to inside the company's walls. Vendors and partners are important constituents; they need to be told that an interim manager is coming on board.

The Marketing department manages many of the company's most strategic partners:

1. Ad agencies
2. PR agencies
3. Web search firms
4. Affiliates
5. Graphic design consultants
6. Research companies
7. Industry analysts
8. Marketing consultants

The Sales department manages critical partnerships that have a direct impact on revenue:

1. OEM partners
2. Distributors
3. Resellers
4. Field service providers
5. Referral networks

The CEO will need to use his best judgment as to how much information he provides to these outside entities about the interim's objectives, especially if it could involve a change such as an agency review, or a move to different sales channel.

Their authority must be made clear to the vendors and partners, and that statement of authority must be **exactly** what the interim and CEO agreed to during the scoping process. If the executive has the authority to recommend a vendor change that message needs to be delivered. If all is well with the vendor relationship and the interim doesn't have authority to make a change, the smart CEO will take pains to compliment the vendor and ease their concern about the transition.

IMPORTANT CUSTOMERS

If the interim will be stepping into a sales executive role the wise CEO will make darn certain that key customers know what's about to happen and why.

This task of talking to your best customers shouldn't be delegated. In fact, the CEO should look at it as an opportunity to connect with his customers.

The approach you take can depend on the circumstances of why the interim is required in the first place. For example, the previous VP of Sales may have been highly respected by your best customers. His or her absence may be causing some problems or ill-will. You'll want to listen to the customer and express that it is because you so value the relationship and their satisfaction level that you have taken extraordinary efforts to fill the gap.

Avoid the temptation to conceal that the interim is temporary, but also avoid discounting their strengths and accomplishments. Speak frankly about the executive's leadership abilities. You want them to feel that they are in good hands once again, and that their interests are top-of-mind.

Properly socializing an interim engagement before it begins contributes greatly to the success of the effort. As one can see from this chapter, socializing an interim executive can be more complex than socializing a new full-time employee. Done properly they can step swiftly and smoothly into the day-to-day flow of the business. Done improperly they will meet with resistance, resentment and confusion.

See Chapter 9 for tips on how to manage an interim manager once the engagement has started.

8.

FINDING ON-DEMAND LEADERS

By Paul Travis

You can't camp out at a Harvard Business School graduation to find a good Interim Leader. Nothing against Harvard in particular; it's just that the kind of leadership described in this book is gained in the real world (many years after graduation) rather than the classroom. So how have others found them?

Like customers, talent is found everywhere you look. You just don't have time to talk to everyone to find the right match.

Thus we offer three avenues for locating the kind of interim talent in marketing and sales from which your organization may benefit:

1. Industry referrals
2. Leadership networks
3. Interim firms

It is worth noting that the leaders we interviewed did **not** view classified advertisements or Monster postings as worthwhile for these mission-critical talent needs. Nothing against these models; they are good ways to get a slew of interest if you want to filter through applications to find a qualified candidate or two who understands the interim model.

Before discussing the three avenues, it is worth underscoring the importance of doing your pre-work in defining the specifics of the engagement. (See Chapter 7). In order to make your search as efficient and effective as possible, you're going to want to give people a clear idea of: what skills you are looking for, the duration of the assignment, any particular background or company experience you require, etc. Equally important to specify are any attributes you **don't** want (e.g. a certain company that you don't want to be associated with).

INDUSTRY REFERRALS

"I'd look within the industry that I was in to find someone who will come up to speed fast."
--Dr. John Castle, University of Washington

Consider yourself lucky if you know somebody who did something very similar with a similar company, who is available, and upon whom you could draw for 3 to 6 months.

More often, the people you know are either fully employed (or trying to pick off **your** good people) or they are happily retired and unmotivated to get back in the saddle.

This is when you contact friends and associates in the industry, looking for someone who can deliver for you that you don't yet know. This can be done by telephone, email, or increasingly through social networking web sites such as LinkedIn.com or Spock.com.

If you aren't finding the right individual, consider using an expanded definition of "industry". In the example above, rather than requiring someone who has led sales teams in telephony, perhaps you really need an individual who understands the dynamics of selling hardware or services to a particular level of enterprise customer.

Another way to "tap by referral" is to approach an **interim**. Even if he/she is already engaged or is not the right fit, they may very well know someone else who could be a match for your needs.

LEADERSHIP NETWORKS

In many cities throughout the U.S. and abroad, there are weekly or monthly "Executive Roundtables" run by dedicated associations such as Vistage (formerly TEC) or by headhunters or coaches in the area.

It is usually pretty easy to track down these groups and the moderator or facilitator. Explore with them the talent pool and you may find that some of the members are in transition and open to an interim leadership role. Your contact may make an introduction or ask you for a write-up that he/she can share by email or at the next meeting.

INTERIM PROVIDER FIRMS

OneAccord is among a small, growing number of organizations that exist to handle this need for interim sales, marketing, and business development leadership -- just as Tatum Partners sprung up to serve companies requiring interim CFO's.

Some firms provide expertise within a specific vertical or geography; others such as OneAccord span many industries and the entire U.S.

Many of the CEO's interviewed for this book with first-hand knowledge in hiring interim leadership felt there was a significant advantage in working with a firm v. an individual:

> *"A firm adds a lot of value because they have a network and expertise; they're able to draw on decades and decades of experience. The broader the base, the more you're getting and the better the value."*
> --Jim Grogan, CEO, Loreto Bay Development Company

In addition to the "power of the network", the interim **firm** provides five key benefits:

> *"The advantage is the firm has back-up interims in case the one you brought on doesn't work out."*
> --Rick Krause, CEO, Boxx Technologies

The most important one is the "insurance policy" of having multiple bodies on the bench, in case the interim isn't succeeding for one reason or another. In most cases, the existing contract is sufficient (or simply amended) and the replacement can step right in.

> *"This is a huge benefit, because they can pass the baton and make a transition where an individual interim that isn't working out might not be so positive about working with his replacement."*
> --Dr. William Sequeira, former COO, ACD Systems

The second benefit is a twist on the insurance policy -- what if the interim really **did** get hit by a bus--or, more applicable these days, carpal tunnel or West Nile Virus?

Third, if the scope of the position expands or highlights another area of opportunity, the interim firm usually has another leader to help out in parallel.

For instance, during an engagement with a $50 million manufacturing company for whom I validated the market for a new product (outside their core competency) I also identified lingering issues in their sales channel. Rather than stretch myself and extend the timelines of the project, I was able to bring in a partner with this specialty.

Fourth, even in situations where another interim is not required, it is quite probable that the interim you hire will have colleagues on which to draw any time he or she needs a reality check from someone equally experienced.

The last benefit is **far** from the least. Namely, the interim firm routinely placing on-demand sales and marketing leadership has knowledge of the process -- not just the process of how placing someone in the saddle but the seasoned understanding that success is not just getting the work done; it's about the power dynamics in the enterprise, points of friction and collaboration between sales and marketing, etc.

Many firms have continuous learning systems to provide their interim talent with templates that have been vetted over time in the marketplace. Often the success of various initiatives will have been discussed between the team members at the interim firm -- so clients benefit from best-in-class comparables/comparisons.

This can be invaluable for the company which has not invested a substantial outside resources in the past.

A common concern is whether the interim firm will really understand the company's business or situation. We've found that many senior executives and board members have this reservation, or they believe that **their** business is distinctly "different" than any other industry in the marketplace.

As I have learned from my sales veteran colleagues at OneAccord, however, the truth is: *sales is sales is sales*. What may differ is product vs. service, business vs. consumer buyer, the length of the sales cycle, and more – but it's always the same process.

Another CEO underscores a why a disciplined professional perspective can be essential for revenue generation.

> *"Marketing and Product Management are the two most difficult disciplines to hire for because there are so many facets to each. And because of the multi-faceted aspect of Marketing and Product Management it's nearly impossible to find an individual that excels at all elements."*

--Rick Krause, CEO, Boxx Technologies

As an example of how the model works for clients, where expectations are managed, and interim services are delivered and value is created, consider this executive's experience:

===

SNAPSHOT

"We originally looked at a six-month engagement with OneAccord—in one year our revenues have increased approximately threefold (300%). Was it worth the money? Yes, no doubt. They are very good at what they do- and they'll be a great resource if you can do something with the knowledge, ideas and expertise they lend."

--David Nilssen, Co-Founder, Guidant Financial Group

===

9.

SELECTING AND MANAGING THE ON-DEMAND LEADER

By Paul Travis

When selecting an interim leader, you'll first want to determine what expertise you're looking for:

- ➤ Domain expertise
- ➤ Fortune 500 sales and marketing process expertise
- ➤ Corporate organizational talent

In a start-up organization, you're likely to need all three. In a more established company, you might have stronger support in one or two of those areas and you need the interim in the third area. It's also important to take into account the skill level of your existing crew:

> *"It really depends on your stage of development, and the **team**, by that I mean the person has to evaluate the team and they also have to be given the authority to decide if the team is sufficient or if they need more help."*
> --Jim Grogan, CEO, Loreto Bay Development Company

Once you've identified domain and experience requirements, there are specific traits and skill-sets that, while desirable in a permanent employee, are **pre-requisite** for a successful interim executive:

- ➤ Personality that is friendly, but not familiar

- ➢ Proven track record of success and extensive background
- ➢ The ability to communicate
- ➢ A *great* (not just good) listener

The most important trait is the ability to communicate. The interim should be an expert both orally and in writing, and be able to *motivate* their team through their communication.

While co-worker respect will be based on the interim's eventual performance at the client company, their initial credibility will be damaged if they don't have the track record to make co-workers sit up and listen.

While all good leaders must be good listeners, the need for this skill is particularly magnified in interim situations. In order for them to quickly assess a company's situation and put together a plan to achieve stated objectives, they must be able to establish rapport with their colleagues, ask the right questions and then listen without prejudice to the responses.

> *"A good leader has to be a good listener. That sounds trite, but it's very difficult, because most leaders are type A's. They're aggressive, they're smart. They think they already know the answer before the person is halfway through the question or the comment, and they're solution-oriented. I think the hardest thing for good people who are in an interim situation is to hold their instincts in check and listen. And listen carefully and gain the respect of their co-workers to have that ability to sincerely listen."*
> --Jim Grogan, CEO, Loreto Bay Development Company

GUIDELINES FOR MANAGING THE ON-DEMAND LEADER

It's important that the interim leader be managed at a high enough level to have credibility. It depends on the organization whether they report to the Board, the CEO or head of sales or marketing, but it's critical to their success.

The principles of managing an On-Demand Leader are the same as your full-time employees (FTE). As discussed in Chapter 7, you'll want to ensure that you agree on written:

- ➢ Objectives
- ➢ Explicitly quantified milestones
- ➢ Measure of results
- ➢ Frequency of your status reports and meetings

There are no hard and fast rules on these principles, as interim managers are veterans who tend to bring 20 to 30 years of experience to the role. Some of the CEO's we talked with mentioned giving on-demand leaders more latitude and the opportunity to effect change, within reason.

As one of my favorite sayings goes: Trust in God, **and** tie your camel.

CERTAIN THINGS CAN'T BE PREDETERMINED OR WRITTEN

Often the interpersonal dynamics that may be a root cause of some of the issues facing the company become apparent to the interim manager in the first month (if not the first week or day).

> *"The human factor has a strong impact on an outsider's ability to hit milestones. An example of this is 'problem employees'. They have a point of view; they have an axe to grind; they're blocking progress. Sometimes interim talent is brought in to make sure that management doesn't have to deal with the fallout. They might be brought in to remove a problem employee, so they'll be the scapegoat."*
> --Dr. William Sequeira, former COO, ACD Systems

More to the point:

> *"There is always bloodshed when organizations change. If you have a new permanent executive, getting rid of the dead wood, they get smeared with a bad image/perception. Interims are great for making change because they're in and out without having to look these people in the eye the next day. Forty percent of an FTE's success is: 'do people like me?' which an interim doesn't worry about."*
> --Alfred den Besten, former Director of Marketing, Avaya Western Europe

THE KNOWLEDGE TRANSFER AND TRANSITION ARE CRITICAL

A great interim engagement can be negated by a poor "baton handoff" at the end -- which is detrimental to you, the interim, their successor, and those in affected departments. So we suggest the following (or some variation thereof) to proactively and responsibly handle this important inflection point.

Sometimes an engagement will entail the interim finding his or her replacement. If this is the case, the interim will have been working with HR or other resources on candidate evaluation through some or all of the engagement.

Regardless, one month or so before the end of the engagement, the "transition timer" begins. Here are some suggestions:

	Day-to-Day Activities	Group Socialization
First half of transition period	50% time dedicated to documenting the job, process, and outstanding issues (to be sure, a good interim has been creating structure all along).	Notify related workgroups and counterparts of pending, **planned** transition.
Last half of transition period	Successor reviews all documentation with interim, embellishing the documentation for clarity.	Successor shadows interim, meeting all workgroups and counterparts. Post-mortems to generate meta-learning.

Make certain to support the budget for this last but certainly not least item. The post-mortem or "debrief" happens at two levels:

1. For the interim and the "dotted-line reporting relationships" to exchange observations about what worked and what could have worked better, with the participation of the successor so that the learning translates into action.
2. For you and the interim to exchange perceived successes and challenges and ideas on how the process could go better in the future (whether or not you ever work with this individual again, **you** want to know how to do it with more success).

What if there is no dedicated successor? Then the documentation becomes all that more important. There will almost always be meetings, even if they are just with you!

FEAR OF LOSS DURING TRANSITION

Your authors believe that the primary reason for slow acceptance of interim management on the revenue side is that CEO's are paranoid that their family jewels will walk away with the interim.

Let's disentangle the concern, because everyone's fears are grounded in something legitimate.

Is your competitor really going to be able to move in on you because it knows what kind of CRM (customer relationship management) system you use? Or because they know you are training your sales team in a certain methodology? Or even that they know who your partners are? Hardly.

The biggest potential leak is the customer database and account knowledge itself. And that will be safeguarded by a good confidentiality agreement when the interim starts. You're more at risk by losing a W-2 Account Executive, which has **nothing** to do with an interim (coming or going).

So you will benefit by keeping the two issues as distinct.

Again, the up-front work is crucial. Gauge the interim on his/her professionalism. If he/she has done other interim work, and plans to do more, then he/she is going to keep confidential information confidential -- just like your lawyer and your accountant does.

In fact, some would say that the interim's perspective and knowledge of multiple companies brings you **extra** value, even if he/she can't explicitly tell you that the reason for choosing Strategy B was because Strategy A failed at their last project!

Case Study: Interim Director of Marketing for a Professional Sports Franchise

Situation: The management team of an Arena Football League lacked the bandwidth and best practices necessary to create a sophisticated and measurable marketing plan. Furthermore, a communication gap existed between the team president, a former engineer, and the other managers who were accustomed to the "run and gun" style of sports operations and sales. These managers were experiencing difficulty producing detailed, measurable plans that met the president's requirements.

Solution: The president retained an interim Director of Marketing for three months to not only create actionable marketing plans for sponsorships and season tickets, but to train the existing managers on how to create acceptable plans in the future.

Result: The interim applied best practices to the planning process and collaborated with the franchise's managers to facilitate knowledge transfer. During the planning process the leader defined market size and segments for the first time to set revenue expectations, defined the stages to the sales cycle and built a financial model that applied metrics to each stage. His models accurately forecast the required lead generation necessary to reach the team's revenue goal. He launched the team's first fan satisfaction survey. At the end of the engagement the franchise had actionable marketing plans for sponsorship and ticket sales, a metrics-driven model to help measure progress, and the knowledge to repeat the process the following year

10.

COMPENSATING THE ON-DEMAND LEADER

By Charles Besondy

We anticipate this chapter will generate a lot of dialogue, which we welcome. Even the executives we interviewed for the book varied widely on certain aspects of compensation. What's important when thinking about the cost and value of interim management is: getting to the "apples to apples" comparison with a full-time employee (FTE). Certainly *direct* costs associated with each resource will be compared, but the foregone revenue opportunity associated with a vacant position or a "marginally-staffed" position must also be considered.

Remember, in most cases, you're not thinking about two different staffing solutions for a full-time position (although elsewhere in this book we suggest there will be companies that look at serial interims as a preferred resource model). Most often, you're trying to fill a temporary gap of some sort—a resource gap, a skill gap, or a bandwidth gap. If the gap didn't exist, *you wouldn't need to consider an interim solution.* If you could fill the gap immediately and cost-effectively with an FTE without exceeding your headcount, you would likely do so in a heartbeat.

Unfortunately for you and your company, most of the time the gaps can't be filled quickly and adequately with an FTE. Fortunately, there is a viable alternative: interim management.

Interim managers are seasoned, highly experienced executives with the ability to work at strategic and tactical levels. While there is no "Blue Book" to refer to in considering the compensation for interim leadership; these capable on-demand leaders carry a price that can be evaluated against traditional human resources-i.e. full-time managers. This chapter will help you understand the costs of an interim engagement and how to calculate the return on investment for yourself, your CFO and the Board.

THE TOTAL COST OF [EMPLOYEE] OWNERSHIP

Chief executives are very accustomed to evaluating the total cost of ownership (TCO) of computer equipment, warehouse equipment office machines, and factory automation systems. They know that the initial price paid for something is a fraction of the real cost to the organization.

Because most CEO's are not accustomed to hiring interim talent, their initial reaction is often to make a quick comparison between the daily rate of the interim and the salary of an FTE. We've observed an interesting two-step mental process that most executives follow when they are considering an interim management solution for the first time.

First, the tendency is to quickly calculate what an interim manager will cost for six months, and compare that to half the annual salary of a full-time manager. For example, let's say the vacant position has a mid-range salary level of $150,000. The interim manager they're considering has a day-rate of $1,750. The executive's math looks something like this:

> ➢ 50% of full-time salary is $75,000
> ➢ Six months (125 days) for an interim at $1,750 is $218,750.

The immediate reaction at this point is usually, "No way, my Board would never go for it." However, as we'll see below, this is not a true comparison.

In the next instant, a savvy CEO will recall the handsome fee they recently paid a management consulting firm to prepare a strategic report and recommendation. The evaluation and report probably took more than three months at hourly fees ranging from $150 to $400 or higher ($1,200/day to $3,200/day).

Suddenly the interim's day-rate isn't looking so high, especially since the interim is actually going to be performing work, not writing reports.

Even though a cost comparison is natural at this juncture, it misses the point: *the position is vacant and likely will be for months* if you persist in recruiting the right FTE. Important work isn't getting done, even if other managers are doing double duty to try and cover the role. If the perfect FTE candidate was standing in your office and entertaining your offer, you wouldn't need to consider alternative leadership to maintain momentum. In reality, however, the gap exists and business momentum is waning.

Therefore, the wise CEO won't make a comparison until he's considered the TCO for a full-time senior manager, including the opportunity cost for the vacant or under-served position. He may run the numbers himself, or ask his CFO.

These are the elements that must be considered:

- Salary
- Performance bonus, which usually has multiple components, one for personal performance and another for corporate performance.
- Benefits and perks, such as an auto, paid parking, club memberships, etc.
- IT equipment and support, including cell phone, laptop, personal printer, and IT services.
- The cost of recruiting, which not only includes the recruiter fee (external or internal), but also any advertising that may have to be done to attract top candidates.
- Interviewing costs, which include the travel costs associated with bringing in candidates from out of town and perhaps flying in the company's executives to interview the candidate in a central location.
- The cost of training, which is often a formalized class or orientation. This also includes costs associated with developing an employee over time and preparing them for advancement.
- The cost of healthcare, Social Security, Medicare, and unemployment insurance (for U.S. companies).
- The hard cost of a severance package and the soft cost of the impact on morale and productivity when a key manager leaves the company.
- The loss of revenue associated with the amount of time the position is vacant. Although this may be the hardest cost component to quantify, it is the most important. Only when you are honest about the impact to the bottom line does the real value of an interim engagement emerge.

Cost Item	New Hire	Interim
Salary	Yes	Fee
Bonus	Yes	None[2]
Benefits & perks	Yes	None
IT	Yes	Yes[3]
Recruiter fee	Yes	None[4]
Interview costs,	Yes	None[5]
Training; orientation	Yes	None[6]
Health insurance	Yes	None
Medicare	Yes	None
Social Security	Yes	None
Severance	Yes	None
Opportunity cost	Variable	Minimal

Table 1: FTE Cost Comparison

Table 1 illustrates the comparison of the TCO of an interim and an FTE. For companies familiar with making decisions about outsourcing, this type of comparison should be familiar. Even after the numbers have been run, the point to remember is this: it isn't how cheaply you put a manager in a chair; it is how quickly you get results and how swiftly you regain momentum to avoid the Zone of Declining Possibilities and Performance Vacuum. (See Introduction chapter).

In Table 2, consider the hypothetical situation where ABC Corporation has a vacancy at the VP of Marketing position. The CEO knows from experience that

---

[2] In some cases, a portion of the interim's fee may be deferred and paid upon achievement of stated objectives. This compensation structure is not suitable for most engagements, however.

[3] IT costs for an interim will fluctuate depending on the circumstances. The required IT support may be the same as a new hire, or a fraction of the costs if the interim is providing his own PC and cell phone, for instance.

[4] If the interim is obtained from an interim provider firm a percentage of the fee will be retained by the firm.

[5] In cases where the interim you're interviewing is not local, you may be able to negotiate that the candidate or his interim firm pays for travel.

[6] If you hire the right interim manager, training will not be required. However, you and the interim may decide it makes good sense to have him attend new employee orientation training.

filling the position will take four to six months. The company is launching a new product during this window, so she's contemplating engaging an interim executive who is available to fill the gap while recruiting progresses. How might the cost comparison look?

Cost Item	New Hire
Salary	$175,000
Bonus @25%	43,750
Benefits & perks	2,500
IT	3,000
Recruiter fee @25%	55,312
Interview costs,	2,000
Training; orientation	500
Health insurance	6,000
Medicare	1,479
Social Security	6,324
Severance, outplacement	43,750
Opportunity cost, 1st year	1,000,000
Employment cost, 1st year	295,865
Employment cost per day, 1st year	1,233
TCO, 1st year	1,295,865
TCO per day, 1st year	5,399
TCO 2nd year	281,803
TCO per day, 2nd year	1,174
TCO for two years.	1,577,668
TCO per day, two-year. average	3,287

Table 2: TCO Hypothetical Example

Here are the details the CEO and her team considered for this scenario:
- ➢ Annual salary: mid-range for the position
- ➢ Bonus: 25% of base salary
- ➢ Benefits & perks: paid parking, health club membership, etc.
- ➢ IT: laptop, cell phone, personal printer for office, IT support overhead charged back to department

- ➤ Recruiter fee: 25% of first year's compensation package
- ➤ Interview costs: a few plane tickets and per diem
- ➤ Training: the per person cost of the company's orientation program
- ➤ Health insurance: The company's share at $500/month
- ➤ Medicare: at 2008 rates
- ➤ Social Security: at 2008 rates
- ➤ Severance: Based on company history the average tenure in the position is 24 months. Severance is three months salary. Severance cost is only factored into the two-year cost of the FTE.
- ➤ Opportunity cost: ABC is introducing a new product that is projected to bring in $10 million a year in incremental revenue. The launch is going to proceed with or without the VP of Marketing; however, the senior management team at ABC has calculated that without a seasoned marketing leader on board during the product launch, the first year's revenue ramp will be slower. The team estimated that $1-$2 million in revenue is at risk if a marketing leader isn't on the team during the next six months.

The true cost of filling this position becomes very apparent here. The employment cost for the first year averages $1,233 per day7. When the opportunity cost is included, the TCO skyrockets to $5,399 per day. Even if the opportunity cost was less, for example, $500,000 the first year, the TOC per day would be $3,316- nearly double the interim manager's rate

In this light, the interim's rate could be $2,000, $2,500, or $3,000 a day for the six-month period and it would still be perfectly justified if he was successful with the product launch for ABC Corporation.

THE INTERIM WORK WEEK

In certain situations, and with some interim managers, the objectives of the engagement can be achieved without the interim being in the office every day and "on the clock." Indeed, in some cases, it may be advantageous for the on-demand leader to *not* be in the office every day if that might serve to distract him from the engagement's goals.

With this in mind, let's look again at ABC's decision-process for bringing in an interim manager at the VP Marketing position for six months. Table 3

---

[7] Based on 240 work days per year.

illustrates several options that can have significant impact on the engagement costs.

In ABC's case, they recognized that the marketing staff was talented but relatively young, needing daily supervision, and that the level of activity required to prepare for the launch would necessitate the interim VP to be at the helm continually. So the decision was made to retain the interim for five days a week for five months, and four days a week for the sixth month of the engagement. The agreed-upon compensation for the engagement was $203,000.

Days per week as VP Marketing at ABC Corporation	6-Month Fee @ $1,750/day
5 days per week	$210,000
4 days per week	$168,000
3 days per week	$126,000

Table 3: Work Week

WHAT FEES CAN YOU EXPECT TO PAY?

There is no "Blue Book" for interim management. The day-rates are set by the individual interim manager or her interim provider firm. As you'd expect, a rate will vary based on skills, experience, availability, the difficulty of the assignment and the measurable value the interim can deliver.

> *"I think it would be really hard to set up a standard [day-rate]. If I were to discuss with someone hiring them for work that they knew was critical to me, I think they would give me the price and say 'take it or leave it'".*
> --Dr. William Sequeira, former COO, ACD Systems

For instance, I have a day-rate base to which I apply numerical factors that adjust the rate based on the type of work I'll be doing, the duration of the engagement, the days per week, commute distance, etc. This is my personal method; other interim leaders will differ.

When applicable, I'm now beginning to factor in the *value* my engagement will deliver for the client. As we saw above in the ABC scenario, the opportunity cost was one million dollars. If I achieve that for a client, I'm certainly justified in negotiating reasonable compensation that reflects the significant value delivered to the client.

Recognizing there is no industry-standard formula for setting day-rates, there is a guideline some on-demand leaders reference when setting their rates.

One school of thought is that an interim's day-rate should be 0.75% to 1.3% of the annual compensation for an FTE. If the total annual compensation is over $125,000, a lower percentage is used. If less than $125,000, a higher percentage is used.

> *"The1% guideline is in line with what I've seen."*
> --Freddie Carroll, Partner, StarTech Early Ventures

How does this compare to our example in Table 2? Multiplying 0.75% times the first year's employment cost equals $2,219 ($295, 865 x 0.75%). Or if we just look at salary, benefits, bonus and insurance the resulting day-rate equivalent is $1,763 ($235,053 x 0.75%). The interim in our example proposed a $1,750 day-rate—right in line with this guideline.

Without accounting for the true employment cost and TCO, however, this 1% rule of thumb can often lead to a misleading conclusion.

> *"That's bogus. That says you'll be paying 3x on an annualized basis. I can see paying up to 1.5x. I might pay the premium for up to 3 months, but after that there is diminishing return. I'm better off paying for a perm [permanent employee]. At more than 6 months, the 1% formula doesn't work."*
> --David Altounian, CEO, iTaggit.com

> *"I don't think the notion [1% guideline] is unreasonable, but this is where the accountant can question the business case. A lot of that could be mitigated by deferred compensation based on performance."*
> --Rick Krause, CEO, Boxx Technologies

DEFERRED COMPENSATION

In our hypothetical example with ABC Corporation, $1 million was the estimated opportunity cost. This was the amount the senior management team at ABC calculated would be at risk if a VP of Marketing was not on the team during the product launch.

If the interim felt the end results were sufficiently under his control, he might propose that a portion of his compensation be deferred and paid based on goal achievement. The deferred portion would see a risk multiplier applied to it.

In our ABC example, the interim's proposed compensation for the six months was $203,000 for the 116 days. However, he could have structured the deal much differently to provide more upside for himself and a lower day-rate for the client.

Knowing that his efforts can impact upwards of $1 million in revenue in the first year, his proposal could look like this:

> ➢ Original engagement compensation = $203,000
> ➢ 20% deferred payment = $40,600
> ➢ Base compensation = $162,400/ Effective day-rate is $1,400.
> ➢ Deferred compensation x a risk factor of 3 = $121,800
> ➢ Total compensation if objectives are met = $284,200
> ($162,400 + $121,800). The effective day-rate is $2,450

Although this example uses cash as the deferred payment, it could just as easily be cash and stock, which may appeal to pre-revenue and early stage companies (but not always to the interim).

In summary, by moving forward quickly to bring in the interim manager, ABC Corporation would have a strong marketing leader in place during a critical time, they'd be in a position to claim that $1 million in incremental revenue that was at risk, and the other marketing activities of the business would purr right along as well. In the last week or so of the engagement, the interim would transition control to the newly-hired VP of Marketing and business momentum would be assured.

TERMS OF PAYMENT

As we mentioned in the previous section, deferred compensation isn't right for every situation and for every interim. Most engagements are more straight-forward about the terms of payment. These terms can vary. Here are a few common payment schedules:

> ➢ A single payment paid when the Statement of Work is executed. This "payment in advance" works well when you've worked with the on-demand leader before and the scope is short and tightly-defined. This

model may bring a lower overall cost to you since the risk and cost of carrying a receivable is removed for the interim manager.

➢ Another frequent alternative is to pay the Interim Manager on a periodic basis. Either conforming to the bi-weekly or monthly payroll plan the organization uses in general, or as milestones called out in the Statement of Work are reached.

➢ A third variation is the incremental payment plan, which expects certain performance objectives to be met and calls for payments in increments during the engagement. This could be 50% at start and 50% upon completion, or, 33% upon execution, 33% at the mid-point and a final 33% upon completion.

In closing, it's important to know your "total cost of ownership" for the position you're trying to fill on an interim basis. Be honest about the opportunity cost associated with **not** having the right person or *any* person in the role. With these numbers in mind you (and the Board), will chart a clear path for negotiating an interim engagement that makes sense for your company and for the on-demand leader.

===

SNAPSHOT

"We like the flat-fee model for 'being there', with a bonus for delivering. For example, we had an interim that had to bring down costs on an operational level, on an economic basis, using more efficient tools. His job was to get 10% cost down in 6 months. Every percentage point additional was bonused [sic]. He brought in a 50% savings and the company was happy to pay! The company gets to pick the interim's brain and save money."

--Alfred den Besten, former Director of Marketing, Avaya Western Europe

===

11.

OIL AND WATER? INTERIMS AND HEADHUNTERS

By Paul Travis

When I schmooze ["attend local business networking functions, meet company leaders and other service professionals, and exchange stories and business cards"] I have found that conversations with independent executive recruiters can feel somewhat "competitive".

At the very least, the typical headhunter may be unable to get his or her head around the concept of interim placement. Why?

In exchange for identifying and pre-qualifying a key management employee, the recruiter typically earns a fee in proportion to the new employee's annual salary -- whether the arrangement involves a pre-paid retainer or a contingency fee. The actual percentage may vary based on the level of competition for talent in the given economic climate. The recruiter usually guarantees that the employee will remain for at least a year, or will place another candidate at no charge.

If the CEO pays a 30% placement fee for a Chief Marketing Officer's (CMO) first-year earnings at a base salary of $200,000 (separate of bonuses, benefits, and equity) he or she wants to amortize that $60,000 over as many months as possible, not to mention additional new-hire costs and other reasons for wanting the CMO to stay a long time.

NO USE FOR SHORT TERM?

So on the one hand, the current headhunter model doesn't benefit from someone who goes inside an organization to solve **short-term** business challenges.

On the other hand, larger companies like Robert Half Accounting have seen the writing on the wall -- just as the Sherpa in Tibet sees the snow level fading year after year, indicating that Global Warming is a trend we can't rationalize our way out of. They have an entire division dedicated to placing executive-level financial experts inside companies on a short-term basis.

That fact is that companies and their human capital needs are changing just as fast as business is changing. Where a new automobile took the manufacturer 2 to 4 years to bring to market 50 years ago, it can now accomplish the same feat in 9 to 18 months.

The November 29, 2007, *Business Week* cites the average tenure of a CMO at 26 months and 44 months for a CEO.

Consider the same CMO who stays just 12 months (on the long side for an interim) instead of 36 months. The amortized recruiting fee overhead becomes $5,000 per month atop the $16,000 monthly salary – which is starting to look like the premium paid for interim engagements.

Accordingly, many good-size companies and some headhunting firms are now placing people on a monthly basis. But this really is a different model: relationship-oriented vs. transactional. It requires account managers for ongoing contact rather than simply "plugging the hole" and moving on.

HOW THE INTERIM CAN HELP THE HEADHUNTER

There is clearly more room for collaboration than initially meets the eye. Here is a frequent dynamic:

> *"Especially with start-up CEO's or founders, there is a perception that the company can attract marquee talent because of its perceived opportunity. Usually due to their own passion for the product or mission, and lack of objectivity with the maturity and desirability or their company, they fail to anticipate the difficulty they can experience recruiting someone away from a major brand in their space."*
> --Gina Peckman, Dynamo Recruiting Inc.

So the CEO believes he or she is seeking a star chef for a 5-star venue, while the recruiter can see that the basics are not in place and the chef wouldn't be caught dead in that kitchen.

Continuing the analogy, the interim comes in and over a 3- or 6- month period, brings the operation up to par -- tidying up the gear, perhaps making a few staffing changes, short-listing the suppliers and generally readying the place for a star to come in and work their magic.

Our firm, OneAccord, has put a "quick sales infrastructure expert" into at least one such company for 3 months, in order to do just this kind of overhauling to make the place attractive to someone the investors swooned over. It ends up being a win/win/win situation.

Bottom line, the recruiter may **never** have been able to obtain the interest of such high-profile talent in the condition the company was in before. Instead, she received a finder's fee for making the introduction – not to mention increasing her likelihood of earning her placement fee.

In order for this to work, it requires a relationship-oriented headhunter – someone who thinks out-of-the-box and values the long-term well-being of their client over chasing a fee for a placement that is unlikely to work out well for the client.

12.

CONCLUSION AND TOP-10 TAKEAWAYS

By Charles Besondy

We sincerely hope that *Leadership on Demand* expanded your perspective. If you're a CEO who hasn't considered interim management as a strategic resource, we trust this book has opened your mind to the possibility. If you've used interim leadership in the past, we hope this book has provided tips and insights on how to be even more successful with the model.

From the beginning, our objective was to create a dialogue and to open minds. We are strong advocates for the practice of interim management, and as such, acknowledge a bias, but we're also seasoned business people who recognize that interim management isn't for every company every time. We believe interim management should be viewed as a powerful strategy for accelerating a company's momentum, sharpening its competitive edge and enabling it to quickly adapt in a rapidly changing economy.

Our top-10 takeaways from this book:

1. AVOID BUSINESS PERFORMANCE GAPS

As discussed in the Introduction, most leaders have a life cycle within an organization. Over time the performance of the leader typically rises and then gradually declines if they are not able to upgrade their skills and effectiveness to meet the rapidly evolving marketplace. To illustrate we identified the Zone of Declining Possibilities and the Performance Vacuum. In either of these two situations, which can extend for months, the entire company or a department suffers from a lack of energy, creativity, direction, and momentum.

Few argue with that observation, but why do U.S. companies invariably tolerate gaps, as painful as they are, until they can fill the opening with an FTE?

Imagine the incremental performance gains for your company if gaps (people, bandwidth, or skills) were filled quickly and on demand.

2. IN SALES OR MARKETING NEARLY EVERYONE IS *INTERIM*

I know some marketing professionals who have worked for the same company for 15 years, but have held 10 different positions. I know others who have worked for 10 companies in 15 years. Years ago, with one company, I reported to five different VP's in a little over four years. Top leaders, such as a CMO, typically are with a company for no more than 26 months.

The point is: rapid change in the marketplace, combined with industry consolidation and technology advances, make it nearly impossible for a marketing or sales leader to be perfectly suited to his or her job for the long-term. Frequent turnover is the outcome. This trend is not only driving up the company's total cost of ownership for FTE's (just look at your company's recruitment expenses for top marketing and sales people over a 4-year period) it is also increasing the frequency of performance gaps.

It's helpful to recognize that in marketing and sales, many are in their position for a relatively short time. When you realize this fact it makes it much easier to consider interim management as a viable resource.

3. INTERIM MANAGEMENT: THE ULTIMATE IN VERSATILITY

Think back on the decisions you frequently have to make when defining a new position or filling an existing position with an FTE. Is there enough work to justify the headcount? What skills do we *really* need today? What talent are we going to need next year in the position? Do we need domain experience or process expertise? Are we looking for a strategic thinker, or a tactical wizard?

These are all valid questions. When you try to balance today's requirements with future needs, the picture of the ideal candidate becomes clear but finding a candidate that is a perfect fit is rare.

Enter the interim manager: an interim engagement can be scoped to fit your exact needs for the period of time in question. One day a week or five days a week; three months or twelve months. In fact, an interim engagement can be filled with a team if that's what it takes to get the right combination of skills and experience.

4. KEYS TO SUCCESS: SCOPE AND SOCIALIZATION

Chapters 5 and 7 are dedicated to these two topics. Defining the scope of the engagement is about accurately defining what you need to have done and your goals, objectives and timelines. It's important to have the direction for the engagement clear in your mind before interviewing interim candidates. You will also benefit by seeking buy-in from your management team as to the key issues and the cost of not moving quickly. Map out the engagement with the interim candidate so he or she can prepare a proposal. The process of "defining the sand box" in detail sets the expectations for both parties and avoids misunderstandings later.

If the interim *and* the engagement are not properly "positioned" within your organization, the early days of the assignment can be bumpy. It is very important that the management team, peers, direct reports, vendors, and sometimes customers be advised in advance that an interim will be coming on- board to address certain opportunities and challenges. The CEO may wish to enlist the help of the Human Resources VP to socialize the engagement in the company.

5. INTERIM MANAGEMENT CAN WORK FOR YOU

Companies large and small can benefit from the strategic use of interim management in marketing and sales. Start-ups in a pre-funding phase are probably the only exception simply because there is seldom money to pay the interim; in this phase the founders are most likely working without pay themselves.

Large companies have many opportunities for applying interim management in marketing and sales because of the sheer number of managers, products, markets. A company with hundreds of products serving dozens of markets is going to have an ever-changing appetite for specific marketing and sales skills that is difficult to maintain with FTE's. A large organization can gain flexibility, speed, and efficiency by augmenting a core of FTE's in marketing and sales with on-demand leadership.

For smaller and mid-market companies, interim management can be the ticket to taking the organization to the next level. As companies grow, they face organizational challenges that are new to them, yet they can't always afford to hire the "big guns" with Fortune 500 experience.

For instance, it's invaluable for a $250 million company, looking to change their channel strategy, to tap an interim sales executive who has done it many times before on a global scale. The interim can work alongside the existing VP of Sales or serve to fill that role during a transition.

By leveraging interim management, companies can set headcount in marketing and sales at lower levels, knowing that they can quickly ramp up the team with on-demand leaders during peak work periods or when gaps occur.

Furthermore, consider that the use of interim managers should not be limited to C-level or VP-level positions. Director-level positions in marketing and sales are equally well-served by an interim strategy. It's not uncommon for an on-demand leader to be engaged in a position for which he is over-qualified. So you can fill a director-level position with a VP-level interim manager—a nice added benefit of the on-demand model.

6. THERE IS A HUGE COST TO DOING NOTHING

If more CEO's recognized the costs associated with keeping the wrong person in a position or allowing a leadership position to remain vacant for months, more companies would be using interim managers in marketing and sales. What competitive challenges aren't being met? What new markets are being ignored? What revenue opportunities are on the backburner? Using interim managers is about marshalling the right resources to achieve the desired result, before it's too late.

7. IT'S NOT THE DAY-RATE, IT'S THE VALUE

Chapter 10 looked closely at the "total cost of ownership" for a full-time executive. When all the costs are considered, an interim's rates are reasonable. But an analysis of direct costs only reveals *part* of the picture. What is the value to the organization of the impact the interim will have during the engagement? Is $1 million in incremental revenue going to be possible because of a more effective product launch? Will the company see a 20% gain in margin because a new sales compensation plan was effective in driving sales of high margin products? Did the market adopt a new product quickly because the product was a tight fit to the needs of the marketplace?

CEO's in the U.K., Belgium and other European countries are ahead of the curve because the use of interim managers in those countries is wide-spread. We believe it's only a matter of time before CEO's here in the States start thinking more frequently about interims for marketing and sales.

8. MIND THE GAP WITH A PARALLEL STAFFING STRATEGY

The authors are not proclaiming the end to full-time employment in marketing and sales. There is a valid need in business for interim talent, consultants, and full-time employees.

Even companies dedicated to the "hire for career" model could access interim management as a gap-closer. As a matter of procedure, when a senior position needs to be filled and it's estimated that three months or more will be required for the recruitment process to bear fruit, they might bring in an interim to fill the vacancy while the search progresses.

Yes, there will be some decisions (like hiring regional sales managers) that the interim should leave for the new hire to make. But there are countless other decisions and tasks that can and should be done by a focused and competent executive while the search goes on. Keep the momentum going: just say no to performance gaps.

9. MANAGE AN INTERIM THE SAME AS AN FTE

An interim should be managed the same as an FTE, and treated the same, too. Managing the interim is relatively easy, because the engagement agreement clearly outlines the objectives, deliverables and milestones (See Chapter 5).

You are encouraged to view the interim as an FTE. As appropriate to their position, they should attend senior management meetings and be invited to step into a Board meeting. They should also be invited to participate in team-building exercises, retreats, and the always popular Friday at Four.[8]

10. INTERIM MANAGERS ARE EASY TO FIND

CEO's we interviewed mostly relied on their business network to locate suitable interim managers. Typically, this means calling another CEO and asking if they know of an available resource.

Interim provider firms can also be an excellent source. They tend to have an impressive stable of C-level and VP-level talent that have made a career choice to work as interim managers. Some firms have offices in multiple cities, which can be a benefit for companies trying to fill gaps in multiple locations.

---

[8] Consult with your HR department to understand how state regulations regarding temporary employees might impact the treatment of your interim manager.

Furthermore, there is comfort in knowing that you can tap into other resources if your chosen interim doesn't work out or becomes unable to work. A partial list of these firms is included in Chapter 13.

Independent interims are also available. Be cautious with independents, however. Many so-called interim managers are really unemployed managers looking for their next full-time job. They could be imminently qualified for the role you're seeking to fill, but they're doing interim work as a financial requirement rather than a career choice. When working with individuals like this, unless they have a long track record as an interim, you have the risk that they'll leave your engagement if a full-time job offer emerges for them across town.

We welcome your comments. A survey is provided in Chapter 14 to facilitate the feedback.

13.

RESOURCES

The following sources of information about interim management are provided for your convenience. These pages are not meant to be a comprehensive list of sources, rather a starting point for learning more about the topic. It is possible other excellent companies and publications exist, but aren't known to the authors. Furthermore, no claims are being made here, explicitly or implicitly, about the accuracy of the information these sources provide, or the quality of service.

Any researcher exploring the topic of interim management quickly learns that the center of the interim management universe appears to be in the U.K. Therefore, most of the interim provider firms and associations are located there, at least for now.

BOOKS

Interim Management, the New Career Choice for Senior Managers
By Dennis Russell

A New Brand of Expertise, How Independent Consultants, Free Agents, and Interim Managers Are Transforming the World of Work
By Marion McGovern and Dennis Russell

ASSOCIATIONS

Interim Management Association (IMA)
IMA members help clients to lead business change, drive core business objectives and relieve pressured management teams.
www.interimmanagement.uk.com/

Institute of Interim Management
The Institute of Interim Management, the pre-eminent professional body for quality standards of accreditation, professional development and best practices.
www.ioim.org.uk/

BLOGS AND FORUMS

enter M – Interim Management
http://entermceo.blogspot.com

Interim Manager's Forum
http://imf-making-a-difference.blogspot.com

Linked Interims
http://www.linkedinterims.com/

OneAccord
http://www.oneaccordcorp.com/writings/blog/

One Riot - One Ranger
http://cbesondy.wordpress.com

INTERIM PROVIDERS (a partial list of US providers)

Boyden Interim Management
http://www.boydeninterim.com/us/

Executive Smarts
http://www.executivesmarts.com

Interim America
http://www.interimamerica.com/

OneAccord LLC
http://www.OneAccordCorp.com

ReefPoint
http://www.reefpointllp.com/

Torch Group
http://www.torchgroup.com

Transition Management Consulting
http://www.transitionceo.com/

Willmark Associates
http://www.willmarkassociates.com

14.

READER SURVEY

The authors invite you to share your perceptions, experiences, and plans, if any, for adopting interim management in marketing and sales. Your input will guide us in our development of additional content on the topic.

We are conducting this brief survey online. The findings will be reported in aggregate only. Your name and company name will not be associated with the results in any way

If you are viewing this page electronically and have an Internet connection, just click the hyperlink to proceed to this book's Website and look for the Reader Survey button. **http://www.leadershipondemand-book.com**

The survey includes the following questions in multiple choice format:

1. In the past two years, has your current organization retained interim managers (C-level, or VP-level, or director-level) for marketing, product management, sales, or business development?

2. In the past two years, has your company used interim managers in other departments besides sales and marketing?

3. If Yes, in what department or function?

4. Have you personally retained an interim manager for sales and marketing in the past two years?

5. What is the likelihood of considering interim managers as an alternative source of temporary leadership in sales and marketing in the next 12 months? (C-, VP-, or director-level). Rate the likelihood on a scale of 0-10 where zero is no likelihood and 10 is extremely likely.

6. If you had a gap in your sales and marketing organization this year what might be the biggest hurdle to using interim managers? Select up to two that best apply.

7. Which of the following topics would you like to see more written about in the near future? Select all that apply.

8. Have you ever served as an interim manager (at any function)?

9. If you answered yes, was the experience a positive one for you?

10. Would you consider being an interim manager (any function) as a career choice within the next year?

11. What statement best describes how the book, *Leadership on Demand*, has impacted your thinking on the topic of interim management for sales and marketing functions? Select one.

12. How likely are you to recommend this book to a friend or colleague? Rate the likelihood on a scale of 0-10 with zero being no likelihood and ten being extremely likely.

13. What is your current title?

14. What is the primary industry of your company or business unit?

15. What was the approximate revenue of your company in 2007?

16. In what state/province are you located? If you're located outside of North America, in what country do you reside?

17. How did you hear about the book, *Leadership On Demand*?

18. Would you like to learn more about a career as an interim manager?

19. Would you like to discuss a possible project or interim engagement with the authors?

20. Would you like to be notified when other articles and publications on this topic are available?

21. If you answered Yes to any of the previous three questions please provide your contact information so one of the authors can reach you.

ABOUT THE AUTHORS

For more information about the authors and to request speaking appearances please visit www.leadershipondemand-book.com.

CHARLES BESONDY

Charles Besondy is recognized as a champion for B2B marketing optimization. If a company suspects their marketing is under-performing or is not aligned with business goals, Mr. Besondy steps in to right the ship. He is especially skilled at solving issues in:

> - Target market selection and sizing
> - Positioning
> - Lead management
> - Marketing strategy and planning
> - Product marketing process

Mr. Besondy is a senior-level "player-leader" who has been an interim manager and consultant since 2001. This is underpinned by 25 years of marketing leadership primarily within small and mid-market software/Web businesses that place an emphasis on action and growth. His experience base spans scores of product categories, technologies and industry segments.

A native of the NW, and a graduate of the University of Oregon, Mr. Besondy has resided in Austin since early 2000. He is a member of the Austin Technology Council and is active in his church. His blog, *One Riot – One Ranger*, (http://cbesondy.wordpress.com) is a leading source of ideas on the topic of interim management.

When not helping clients boost their marketing performance he can be found on long walks through the wilderness looking for his golf ball. Mr. Besondy can be reached at cbesondy@leadership-on-demand.com.

PAUL TRAVIS

From his 25 years of experience in high technology, marketing, and consulting, Paul Travis has developed two core specialties:

> Determining and developing the right product(s) for the target market (full lifecycle Product Marketing)
> Establishing appropriate marketing infrastructure to profitably attract/retain customers (Analytics to CRM)

Mr. Travis began project and interim consulting in 2000, having recognized that small- and mid-market organizations needed the same things that had made him successful with larger private and public companies.

In his prior corporate marketing career, Mr. Travis built a ten-person marketing team as VP Marketing at safety/security concern Net Nanny Software Inc. There he oversaw the launch of two consumer products and the BioPassword enterprise product (later spun off). At analytics provider Marketwave Corporation, his shift of focus and licensing structure into the enterprise space increased the company's run rate by 1,000% in just nine months -- prompting a $77 million competitive acquisition. He currently serves as a board member of 2 privately held companies. He concentrates on three verticals: *high technology, food and beverage, and manufacturing.*

Mr. Travis is a Microsoft Alumni Network member; is President of the Institute of Management Consultants (IMC) Pacific NW Chapter; and co-founded the Seattle Chapter of the CRM Association. He completed the Brand Management Executive Program at Harvard Business School and received his

Bachelor's Degree in Computer Science & Mathematics from the University of Illinois at Urbana-Champaign.

Mr. Travis resides with his wife and two children on Bainbridge Island (due west of Seattle, Washington). He enjoys hiking, camping, racquetball, percussion, and singing in the shower. Mr. Travis can be reached at ptravis@leadership-on-demand.com.

THERESA HEATH

With over 25 years of sales and marketing experience, Ms. Heath is a strategist and sales turnaround expert with an innate ability to swiftly diagnose root causes and underlying issues in revenue shortfall situations and then develop  and implement strategies that quickly transform into positive sales trends.

Ms. Heath has deep and broad functional knowledge ranging from Fortune 100 companies to venture-backed startups, executing at the C-suite and board level the past 12 years. Her experience spans pharmaceuticals, diagnostics, medical devices and information technology. Ms. Heath combines a strong entrepreneurial orientation with a collaborative leadership style.

Ms. Heath focuses her attention on areas where she can make the greatest contribution:

- ➢ Sales and Marketing Leadership
- ➢ Strategic Planning and Implementation
- ➢ Business Development
- ➢ Strategic Alliances and Partnerships

Ms. Heath graduated cum laude with a Bachelor's of Science degree in Business Administration from Arizona State University. She is a Member of Standard & Poor's Vista Research Society of Industry Leaders and is a volunteer in the mentoring program for Arizona State University's Technopolis entrepreneurial program. A wife and mother of two teenage girls, she enjoys travel, yoga/Pilates, music, and cooking for family and friends. Ms. Heath can be reached at theath@leadership-on-demand.com.

FIGURES AND TABLES

INDEX